MEAT LOGIC

Why Do We Eat Animals?

CHARLES HORN

ISBN: 1499379242
ISBN-13: 978-1499379242

To liberty and justice for all

CONTENTS

PREFACE

Despite the moral dilemma surrounding the issue, eating animal products is thought of as normal while people who don't eat such products are thought of as abnormal. People so assuredly provide their rationalizations for why eating animals is justified, and each person seemingly has a different rationalization than the next. I found myself wondering what people would think if they examined all of these rationalizations together in one place. Would it reinforce their own views, or challenge them?

A complete discussion of the topic, however, requires some philosophical background, so I have included an overview of some of the philosophical thought regarding animals and morality.

It should be noted that while this book deals with issues of morality, the word is not meant in any preachy or religious way. What this book is really about is logic and rationality. Do our thoughts and actions stand up to rational scrutiny? If not, can this be shown? If there are errors in our thought process, can they be illuminated? These are some of the questions that I hope to answer.

It should also be noted that I do not claim to be addressing all aspects of animal rights. Even with humans, there are some areas of morality and hypothetical extreme case examples where morality isn't 100% clear, but that does not negate morality or prevent us from being able to reason through the morality of everyday living. For most day-to-day cases, morality is much more clear, and that is what I focus on here, specifically in regard to eating animals.

In terms of structure, this book consists of two main parts, the first being the philosophical background regarding animals and morality, with a specific focus on eating, and the second being a collection of all of the different rationalizations we humans generally give for eating animals. It is quite possible that I have missed some, but other seemingly different rationalizations oftentimes can be broken down as some combination or variation of the rationalizations listed here. Finally, links to any factual material stated within the main body of the book can be found in the notes section at the end.

INTRODUCTION

A majority of people eat animals (and we will use the phrase "eat animals" to mean any products made from animals, including the flesh of animals, as well as dairy and eggs). According to a 2012 Gallup poll, only 2% of U.S. adults said that they do not eat any animals. Most people never even question the eating of animals: it's how they were raised, it tastes good, everyone else is doing it, and you get a free toy with every Happy Meal! Some people even make fun of those who don't eat animals, calling them kooks and extremists.

But just because we don't question something doesn't mean it's right. At one point in history, people didn't question human sacrifice. For much of history, people did not question human slavery. Morality today requires a stronger justification than just, "But that's the way we've always done things." Ultimately, there needs to be a valid moral justification for any of our actions in life.

So what is the moral justification for eating animals? Most people generally think such a question is absurd to begin with, but if pressed to answer they tend to provide one of a number of rationalizations. In this book, we examine these rationalizations and put them to the test to see how well they stand up to rational scrutiny.

But first let's talk a little philosophy...

PART I: PHILOSOPHY AND ANIMALS

In this section we present some of the philosophical thought concerning animals, and attempt to apply it to the case of eating. Numerous books are listed in the bibliography for anyone wishing to explore the topic further.

BIAS AND MISCONCEPTIONS

Our Historical Bias

Before even beginning on any discussion about how we should or should not treat animals, the first thing we must note is that we all have a long-standing bias toward treating animals as resources to be used by humans as they see fit.

This bias goes back thousands of years and runs deep in the heart of our civilization. Both Judeo-Christian beliefs and Greek philosophy, the two historic pillars of Western civilization, treat animals as made for the sake of man.

The Old Testament gives man "dominion over the fishes of the sea, and over the fowl of the air, and over every living thing that moveth upon the earth." Man is unique, made in God's image, the central figure of creation, and set apart and above from the other animals.

Greek philosophers believed that animals existed to serve man. Aristotle, one of the most famous Greek philosophers, wrote, "Since nature makes nothing purposeless or in vain, it is undeniably true that she has made all animals for the sake of man."

There have been opposing voices against such treatment of animals throughout history. To name only a quick few, Greek philosopher Pythagorus was against such a view, as was Leonardo da Vinci and Ghandi. Obviously these opposing voices did not prevail. The views of the Bible and Aristotle continue to hold sway to this day.

A truly low point for animals came in the 1600s when French philosopher René Descartes argued that animals had no consciousness and were simply automata, machine-like things that might act like they had consciousness or might look like they were in pain but really it could all be explained away in purely mechanistic terms. Descartes and other scientists would dissect live animals and make fun of anyone who felt bad for the animals.

Finally, in the mid 1800s, Darwin's theory of evolution completely upended the notion that man was separate from the animals. Evolution tells us that our human-centric way of thinking is unwarranted, which means we need to rethink the subject of our relationship to animals from scratch. Humans are in fact animals themselves, and non-human animals do not merely exist for the sake of humans, but rather they happen to inhabit the same planet and share common ancestors.

However, given our deep human-centric bias, anything suggesting otherwise tends to be furiously rejected for as long as possible, so even though evolution was finally accepted as scientific fact, its full ramifications have still not made it into the public sphere and changed our old ways of thinking yet.

At a bare minimum, when reading and thinking upon the subject of animals, we should at least recognize and be aware of our deep-seated historical bias toward thinking that animals exist for the sake of man. And we should have the strength of character to continually force ourselves to question such thinking.

A Few Misconceptions Regarding Animals

Together with our historical bias, many of us still have a number of deep misconceptions about animals, so it is important to correct some of them before going on.

Sentience

When discussing morality with regard to non-human animals, the word sentience quickly comes up. Sentience is the capacity to feel and have subjective experiences. Sentient beings are aware and can subjectively feel varying degrees of pain, pleasure, joy, happiness, desire, fear, loneliness, boredom, frustration, and so on. Sentience is relevant to morality because if a living being is not actually aware and can not feel, then while we may respect the biological life of the being, when we act on it we are not causing it pain or forcefully imposing our will over its will. A non-sentient being simply reacts to stimuli but does not have a subjective awareness and will of its own, or its own feelings and desires.

Science has progressed by leaps and bounds since the 1600s and most of us should now know that Descartes' supposition that animals have no consciousness and don't feel pain is completely false. Anatomy and the theory of evolution show how animals are just way too similar to humans for Descartes' theory to stand up to any reason. If animals show signs of consciousness or signs of pain, which they do in the very same ways we do, the only reasonable conclusion given our scientific knowledge is that they are indeed conscious and feel pain, just as we are conscious and feel pain.

If one wants to claim that animals do not experience pain or do not have any intelligence or do not have consciousness or are not sentient, the burden of proof now lies solely with that person, and not on the animal. Evolution has irrevocably changed the dynamic. It is no longer anthropomorphism for us to believe that animals have these qualities. In fact, just the opposite. It is now a clear irrational prejudice and bias in favor of humans to believe without proof that only humans possess these qualities, because evolution and anatomy suggest otherwise.

According to our current knowledge, all vertebrate animals (including fishes, birds, and mammals) are sentient to various degrees, and so are some advanced invertebrate animals such as the octopus and squid.

Higher Level Abilities

As we move up the evolutionary scale, the levels of sentience and intellect generally increase, to the point where humans have a level of reasoning ability much more advanced than other animals. However, because of our natural prejudice, we also tend to greatly discount the abilities of all other animals, often dismissing their abilities entirely.

One example is with the notion of self-awareness. This is usually tested by a mirror test to see if the animal can recognize itself as an individual in the mirror (although many scientists have pointed to various drawbacks in relying too heavily on this one test, especially given that many animals rely more on smell than sight). All of the great apes have passed this test, as well as some other animals such as dolphins, orcas, elephants, and magpies. Pigs can use mirrors to find hidden food, but have not yet been seen to definitively pass. Humans do not generally pass until they are between 18 and 24 months old.

Some people discount animals who are not able to pass the mirror test. However, not having self-awareness does not mean not having any kind of individual awareness. Even if animals don't know their individual names, they still know when something is affecting their body. In fact, there is a notion of a Me-self and an I-self. Animals who may not have the more advanced version of self-awareness still have the less advanced version.

Another example is with temporal self-awareness. Almost all humans have a well-defined sense of past and future and some people will discount animals entirely because they do not match up to our abilities. However, any animal who shows fear must have some level of temporal self-awareness. Any animal who shows avoidance of previously remembered pain must have some level of temporal self-awareness. Any animal who hides food must have some level of temporal self-awareness. Any animal who shows anticipation for future pleasure must have some level of temporal self awareness. There is clearly a form of temporal self-awareness going on in animals even if it does not match up to the level of humans.

Further examples include language, tool usage, complex emotions, and a sense of death, which were all thought of as being unique to man until it was proven wrong. Research has now shown that animals even display aspects of moral behavior, such as honesty, guilt, and altruism.

Of course, it should be pointed out that regardless of any differences in reasoning ability there is no reason to believe that higher intelligence should be linked to a greater ability to feel emotions or pain. For all we know, some emotions may even be experienced to a greater degree in some animals than in humans.

Evolution has shown us that differences between humans and other animals are one of degree, not of kind. All sentient animals feel pleasure and pain and have emotions and their own conscious desires, but we have to be careful even when we are talking about more advanced cognitive abilities not to discount other animals entirely. To do so merely betrays our historical bias and prejudice.

THE PHILOSOPHICAL BASIS FOR ANIMAL RIGHTS

We now present a brief introduction to some of the important philosophical thoughts concerning animals today.

Moral Status

Something has "moral status" if we should include it in our moral thinking for its own sake. In other words, it is not an "it" at all, but rather a someone and not a thing. Do animals have moral status? Some people actually think that they don't, but there appears to be no rational basis for such a view. If a being is sentient and can feel pain, that should already be reason enough for its own sake to not wish to cause that being unnecessary pain. The reason not to be cruel to an animal is not just because the cruelty will affect humans (either ourselves or others); it is because the cruelty will affect the animal.

Most people now believe that non-human animals have moral status (although we shall see that people still mostly act as if they don't). But how should an animal's moral status compare to that of a human? Here are three possible ways to answer that question.

Equal Consideration

In his book, *Animal Liberation*, Peter Singer provided a philosophical basis for the equal consideration of animals. Singer popularized the idea that ***speciesism***, which is discrimination based on species membership, is simply another form of unwarranted discrimination such as racism or sexism.

Many people get confused and think he is saying that animals are equal to humans in every way, so let us expand a bit on what is really being said. The moral case against discrimination such as racism and sexism is not that all people are exactly the same. People of different colors obviously look different from each other and men and women have many obvious differences as well. These differences can even lead to different rights, such as for example whether or not a woman has the right to an abortion, or whether or not the physically disabled have the right to ramps in order to be able to enter buildings.

So when we talk about equality, it isn't about equal treatment; it is about equal consideration of interests. In other words, we should consider the interests of others equally, regardless of race, sex, and furthermore intelligence, moral capacity, height, physical strength, physical ability, sexual orientation, and so on.

If that is to be a valid moral guiding principle, there appears to be no justifiable reason that such equal consideration should not extend to nonhumans as well. When we ignore that principle for animals we are perpetrating the discrimination of speciesism, a prejudice and bias of our own species against the other species. Such discrimination should be condemned, just as we should condemn racism and sexism.

Now, what does it mean to give equal consideration to animals? Well, one thing that all sentient beings share is the ability to feel pain and suffering. So one important way in which to give equal consideration to animals is to treat an animal's pain with the same consideration as one would treat a human's pain.

That isn't to say that the pains are always equivalent for a human and an animal. A large animal might have a thick hide and feel less pain than a human if struck the same blow. A human might experience more terror than an animal in some situations, or less terror than an animal in other situations. But to the extent that one can measure all of these factors, one should treat the equivalent levels of pain in an animal and a human the same, and not just say that a human's pain is always more important than a non-human animal's pain. Saying that a human's pain is always more important is pure speciesism and should be condemned, just as we should condemn racism and sexism.

Unequal Consideration – Sliding Scale

Opponents of the equal consideration position argue that humans lead richer lives because of their higher brain capacity and thus should be accorded greater consideration. While they agree that animals have moral status, they argue that animals should not be given equal consideration, but rather the consideration should be weighted on a sliding scale roughly according to where the animal stands on the evolutionary scale. In other words, most weight should be given to humans, then chimpanzees, mammals (in general) more than birds, birds more than reptiles, and so on down the scale.

This view may sound reasonable at first glance, but it is quite problematic for a number of reasons. The first thing one should notice is that it is arguing for the exact same principle we hold to be discriminatory in humans. If higher brain capacity or leading richer lives deserves a higher weighting, then why don't we accord higher weightings within humanity to humans with higher brain capacity or humans who lead richer lives? Most people would strongly condemn such a weighting. Plus, as we already saw, equal consideration already allows for the consideration that humans might experience a deeper sense of pain or suffering in some situations than an animal. Why do we need an extra level of weighting on top of that?

Another serious problem with the sliding scale model is that the weighting is not specified, so it is completely open to interpretation according to our own bias. For example, if the unequal consideration leads us to conclude that the animal always loses out to a human, it seems that this was just a verbal machination to lead to our desired speciesism result. We effectively reach the point of saying that animals are here to do with as we please, without having to come right out and say it. At its extreme, it comes off similar to what Chief Justice Roger Taney once said about African Americans at a low point in U.S. history, ruling that they were, "so far inferior, that they had no rights which the white man was bound to respect."

It seems to us that the sliding scale model is a form of evasion by trying to switch the question. It is almost as if when someone brings up the question of animal rights, we hear the question as, "In an emergency where you could only save one of the two, would you save the animal or the human?" We answer to ourselves, "The human, of course," and then think all is right with the world. But that isn't the question. The question is, "In my regular day-to-day living, should I ever cause unnecessary harm to a human or should I ever cause unnecessary harm to an animal?" to which the answer should be "Neither, of course."

Most humans may indeed lead richer lives than non-human animals, but it seems to us that the sliding scale model is simply a form of evasion, answering the question of who you save in an emergency rather than how you should act on a regular day-to-day basis. (As an aside, it should be noted that in some emergency cases one might even wish to save the animal instead of a particularly evil human, such as a mass murderer.)

This switching of questions is also described in the book *Introduction to Animal Rights: Your Child or the Dog?* by Gary L. Francione, who points out that while we may favor the human over the animal in situations of true emergency or conflict, that does not mean we are allowed to manufacture the conflict or emergency in the first place. Just as in the case of a young child and a very old person, we may favor saving the young child over the very old person in an emergency, but that does not mean we should devalue the moral status of old people in our regular day-to-day life. Or similarly, we may choose in an emergency to save someone we know over someone we don't know, but that does not mean we get to devalue the moral status of people we don't know in our regular day-to-day life.

Strong Rights

While opponents of animal rights argue for unequal consideration for animals, saying that equal consideration goes too far, many proponents of animal rights point out that equal consideration does not go far enough. There are some core basic rights that individuals possess which should not be overridden regardless of what anyone else wants, and it would be speciesism to provide such core basic rights only to humans but not other species. Just as an individual human should not be killed or forced into slavery even if it could provide a net benefit to a larger group of people, individual animals should enjoy those same strong rights at least in terms of their life and liberty. We should not be able to override such core basic rights, even though it could lead to some benefits for humans. It is the individual's life and liberty; it is not ours to take. Tom Regan was the first person to develop a solid philosophical grounding for such a view, in his landmark book *The Case for Animal Rights*.

It is beyond the scope of this book to go into much detail, but in general philosophical terms Regan utilizes a notion of inherent value applied to moral agents and moral patients. Moral agents are those like us who have the capacity to act rationally and make proper moral decisions, while moral patients are those who don't have that capacity (e.g., mentally impaired humans, non-human animals). Regan describes a rights philosophical framework where moral agents should have an equal respect for the inherent value of both other moral agents as well as moral patients. That inherent value is not something that should be overridden by any cost benefit analysis involving others. Regan rigorously shows how such a philosophical framework leads to a consistency and generality and has further characteristics that are more favorable as compared to competing philosophical frameworks.

Others have also been working on legal rights for animals. For example, attorney Steven M. Wise has been working to break the species barrier within the law, starting with the most highly intelligent animals. His work aims to provide them with the same legal rights as children or mentally disabled people, who may not enjoy full rights within society but at least have limited rights and protections against their body and liberty.

Finally, in perhaps the most straightforward and powerful argument for animal rights, law professor Gary L. Francione argues that all sentient animals must at least have the basic right to not be treated as property. Otherwise, their interests will always come second to those of their property owner.

In his groundbreaking book, *Introduction to Animal Rights: Your Child or the Dog?*, Francione uses a straightforward and extremely powerful argument to show that once we consider animals to have moral status, it follows from basic principles of equality – specifically, the principle of treating like cases alike – that all sentient animals, independent of their mental capacities, must have the basic right to not be someone else's property, just as all sentient humans, independent of their mental capacities, have the basic right to not be someone else's property. This is not a matter of us feeling compassion toward animals or seeing them as beautiful creatures of nature to be protected, but rather it is a strict matter of justice. Justice demands it.

Some people think that animal rights is a crazy utopian dream that will never happen, but the abolishment of human slavery was once thought to be a crazy utopian dream as well. If we claim to be against prejudice, we must also be against the prejudice of speciesism, and animal slavery must end. In fact, we are already beginning to move toward animal rights. India has now legally declared dolphins and other cetaceans to be "non-human persons," thus banning their captivity.

A FEW PROBLEMS WITH THE ARGUMENTS FOR SPECIESISM

Those who argue for unequal consideration for animals generally argue that humans have some higher cognitive level trait which other animals do not possess and that justifies our unequal consideration. This higher level cognitive trait might be self-awareness, or temporal self-awareness, or moral reasoning, or autonomy, or language, or tool use, or leading richer lives, or any of a number of other higher level cognitive traits. Whichever traits are put forward, there tends to be a few logical inconsistencies with these arguments that come up over and over again. We are going to see these issues throughout the rest of the book, so we will discuss them in a little more detail here.

Mentally Impaired Humans

Any higher level cognitive trait that is supposed to distinguish between humans and other animals also does not exist in many humans as well (e.g., the severely mentally impaired, the senile, babies). If one argues to distinguish between humans and animals based on these traits, then logically one is arguing to distinguish between humans who don't possess these traits either. If we argue that we have the moral right to make animals our slaves or to cause them unnecessary pain and suffering or to kill and eat animals because they don't possess a certain trait, then we are arguing that we have the moral right to do those things to these humans as well.

In the case of babies it is argued that they will possess the trait in the future. But what does that say about a baby who we knew would not live to reach that point? Also, if we hold that reasoning, we may also have to hold that a new

18

fetus should have the same rights as a born person because the fetus will become a person in the future. Although in the case of the fetus there is the mother to consider as well.

Some people argue that we give rights to mentally impaired humans not for their own sake, but for the feelings of their relatives. But that hardly sounds right, and obviously that would not apply to someone who was an orphan and had no family.

Another argument is that medical advancements might cure these impaired humans one day. But there are plenty of humans who are mentally impaired to such a point where they will certainly remain extremely mentally impaired for their entire lives.

Some people argue that mentally impaired humans are viewed by us differently than non-human animals, which gives us the right to treat them differently. But that is simply saying that we are speciesist, therefore we are allowed to be speciesist. Imagine saying that we view black people differently than whites or men differently than women and therefore are allowed to treat them differently.

Another argument is that mentally impaired humans are treated differently than non-human animals because they belong to a species that has the higher level ability. This is once again unsatisfying as it is purely by definition. There is no logical rhyme or reason why it should work by species rather than by individual. Imagine being told by someone that males have greater moral status because of their size and strength. We tell them that not only is that reason irrelevant to moral status, but some women are bigger and stronger than some men. The response we receive back is that it works by size and strength of the overall sex rather than individuals and those smaller men enjoy the greater moral status because they belong to the sex with greater size and strength. Not only would we find that answer completely unsatisfying, we would see it as confirming the prejudice of sexism. It is simply dishonest intellectual machination on the part of the prejudiced person to obtain the result they want.

Yet another argument is that mentally impaired humans are given rights because they belong to a moral society who has the idea of rights. But the fact that a society has an idea of something is not connected to where that idea applies, or even if that idea is true or not. For example, we don't say that the idea of gravity only arises within human society so gravity does not apply outside of humans. And we don't say that the reason gravity exists in society is that society has the idea of gravity. Whether gravity exists or not is independent of the idea of gravity. Now, one might attempt to argue that human morality and rights are a human construct and so humans have the power to set the rules as they like, but if it is done arbitrarily to include all humans and exclude all nonhumans purely by definition alone, then it is clearly prejudicial. It is the logical equivalent of hanging a "No Nonhumans Allowed" sign when it comes to morality and giving or acknowledging rights.

Finally, some people argue that there is simply a different morality standard toward other humans than toward non-human animals. But if one can just decide to define morality differently, then one could just as easily decide to define morality toward white people to be different from morality toward black people, or morality toward men to be different from morality toward women.

Ultimately one is left only with the unsatisfying slippery slope argument, that we only grant these mentally impaired humans rights because we are worried about where to draw the line. This however is a purely speciesist argument in itself, as we prejudicially apply it in favor of our own species and against every other species. The logical inconsistency remains regardless.

Dogs and Cats

Dogs and cats show us that in reality we find this higher level cognitive trait position to be logically inconsistent. Dogs and cats do not possess higher level cognitive traits and yet most of us utterly reject the notion that we have the moral justification to kill and eat them. Not only do we reject it, we find it barbaric. And furthermore it does not matter if it's our own dog or some theoretical dog we will never even meet. We seem to hold that there is an intrinsic worth to animals regardless of whether or not they meet our criteria for higher cognitive level traits.

It is true that our social conditioning allows many of us to hold the blatant inconsistency in our heads that dogs and cats have intrinsic worth while other animals can be assigned to be our food, and it is also true that other parts of the world eat dogs and cats and value different animals instead, but still our feelings regarding dogs and cats show that the higher level trait argument is logically inconsistent. One would have to argue that we don't actually hold dogs and cats to be of value on their own and their true value comes only from the feelings of humans. In essence, we would have to go all the way back and argue that animals don't even have any moral status whatsoever in order to fix this logical inconsistency.

Neanderthals

Neanderthals are the extinct caveman species most closely

related to humans. A hypothetical question to pose to someone arguing the higher level traits position is where would Neanderthals fall in their moral considerations? We seem to be trying so hard to maintain a strict wall of separation between humans and every other species. How would we react if we found a long lost group of Neanderthals? Would the extreme closeness of our abilities finally force us to confront our speciesism and recognize that Neanderthals should be treated equally as well?

Future Man

An even more important hypothetical to consider, in our opinion, is a future evolved species of man. Evolution did not go on for billions of years to just suddenly stop. It is perfectly reasonable to suppose a time in the future when a more advanced species will evolve who will take over being in charge.

Such future evolved man could make the exact same higher level cognitive trait argument using an even higher cognitive threshold, in which case if we argue that sentient animals deserve no rights then we are also arguing that future man has the moral authority to enslave and kill and eat Homo sapiens.

One might argue that future man would surely have to recognize that we passed a high cognitive threshold even though we were not at the same high level as them, but one must remember that they get to set the rules, not us. If it is moral for us to completely discount the lower cognitive abilities of sentient animals, then it must also be moral if future man decides to set the cognitive threshold higher than our abilities and thus completely discounts our lower cognitive abilities. It would in effect be perfectly okay for them to say "It's just a Homo sapien" the same way many of us say "It's just an animal."

This thought experiment has compelling importance, as it for the first time forces us to consider a situation where our species is not at the top. Our deep-seated historical bias has been to consider humans as the center of the universe. This perfectly reasonable thought experiment forces us to consider if our arguments and positions would change if the shoe was on the other foot, as it were.

It seems fairly certain that most people arguing the higher level cognitive traits position would quickly find themselves changing their position from unequal consideration to strong rights.

Space Aliens

A similar hypothetical can be made for space aliens. If a person were abducted by advanced aliens, and that person did not believe in any rights for animals, it would seem they would have very little basis to complain about any anal probing they might receive. After all, that person holds the position that a more advanced species has the moral right to enslave or exploit or kill and eat a lower species. Although we have expressed this space aliens hypothetical in a humorous way, it is nevertheless instructive.

Answering the Wrong Question

Ultimately, as we have noted previously, the higher level cognitive traits position is faulty because it is in fact answering a different question. We can see this even within humanity. People who have a higher degree of higher level cognitive traits generally have more opportunities. They will generally excel in their studies, get higher grades, get into better universities, get more advanced degrees, and in general get better and higher paying jobs. But never for a moment do we consider making slaves of people who have a lower degree of higher level cognitive traits. And never for a moment do we consider killing and eating them. For those core basic issues we seek out the lowest common denominator. It is the essence of our guiding principle of equality for all. We don't desperately seek out ways of differentiation so that we can discount others completely.

In an emergency where we can only save one of two people, we may indeed decide to save an Einstein over a mentally impaired person, but we do not apply that to everyday living. In everyday living, everyone is supposed to be treated equal. The higher level cognitive traits position is most definitely not the position we take on everyday living, and especially not on core basic everyday issues of whether we have the right to make someone our slave or to cause them pain and suffering or to kill and eat them.

In fact, whenever we think in terms of an emergency no-win situation, proceed to rank worths based on it, and then carry those rankings over to everyday life, we are using a classic thought process of prejudice. A mentally impaired person should enjoy the very same basic rights as an abled person. We should equally oppose discriminating against either of them. We should equally oppose enslaving either of them. We should equally oppose treating either of them as property or as a resource for our own ends. This should be true regardless of our emergency situation ranking.

Similarly with sentient animals, who are all individuals in their own right. We should equally oppose discriminating against any of them. We should equally oppose our enslaving any of them. We should equally oppose treating any of them as property or as a resource for our own ends. This should be true regardless of our emergency situation ranking.

Within humanity, we seem to know not to confuse the emergency no-win situation with the case of everyday living. When it comes to animals, however, we seem to have amazing difficulty with our thought process. We must stop confusing the two situations. They are two different questions entirely. It is faulty thinking to confuse the two.

IN TERMS OF EATING

We are now getting close to attempting a discussion about the morality of eating animals. But first we need to know more about animal agriculture.

Animal Agriculture

Since our focus is on eating, we need to discuss how animals reach our plate. For efficiency and scale and profit, almost all farmed animals today are raised in factory farms. The treatment of animals in factory farms and slaughterhouses has been well documented using unbiased information provided by the government and the animal agriculture industry itself, as well as first-hand reporting. The description below represents only a tiny overview of standard industry practices.

Most people are unaware that female cows provide milk only when they have babies, as the milk is produced for feeding their own calves. To maximize milk production, cows are therefore impregnated, and after the birth the calf is immediately dragged away from his or her mother. That cycle is repeated continuously until the mother can no longer produce enough milk to industry standards, at which point she is sent off to slaughter, living only about four years of her twenty to twenty five year natural lifespan. If any calf is male, he is either immediately killed or raised briefly for veal. Veal calves are intentionally fed a nutritionally-deficient diet, may be kept in the dark for their entire short lives, and are confined to the point where they can not even get up and turn around. The goal is to keep the meat pale and soft. Veal calves are killed anywhere between a few days up to six months after birth. Non-veal cattle raised for their meat are killed anywhere between ten to eighteen months after birth.

Female breeder pigs live a life of such confinement that they are not even able to turn around in their concrete and steel cages. The goal is to get impregnated, create more pigs, repeat, and finally get sent off to slaughter after three to five years. The males do not get off easy either, being castrated without anesthesia and living in extremely overcrowded pens. Tails and teeth are cut without anesthesia as well. Piglets who are not growing fast enough are killed immediately by being swung by their legs and bashed onto the concrete floor, a process known as "thumping." The remaining pigs are sent to slaughter after only six months of their ten to twelve year natural lifespan.

The trip to slaughter for cows and pigs is extremely crowded and arduous, involves very rough handling, and is lacking in rest, food, water, and protection from the elements. Although they are supposed to be stunned unconscious before being hoisted upside down in the air to have their throats cut and bleed to death, very often the stunning is not applied appropriately and the animal struggles and dies fully conscious, already being skinned and dismembered while they are still alive. It is not economical to stop the factory line.

Egg-laying hens are kept in incredibly cramped conditions (given a space smaller than a sheet of paper) where they can't even stretch their wings. They are kept in the dark for long periods and starved for long periods. Their beaks are partially seared off with a hot blade and they are worked in overcrowded conditions laying eggs at an accelerated rate until their bodies are spent within one or two years. Finally they are slaughtered, their throats slit while they are fully conscious. Male chicks are deemed useless from the start because they can't lay eggs, so they are killed on their first day of life, either through suffocation in garbage bags, electrocution, gassing, or by being chopped up alive in a blender. Most people are not aware of that. Or that the words "free-range" or "cage free" are practically meaningless because these terms do not mean what people think they mean (and we will discuss this in detail in Chapter 30).

Broiler chickens, the kind grown for their flesh, are also kept in incredibly overcrowded conditions and have their beaks partially seared off with a hot blade. They are killed fully conscious at around six weeks. A chicken's natural lifespan can be eight years or more. In fact, many of the farmed animals we have been discussing are no longer even the animals they once were. They have been selectively bred for quick massive unsustainable growth. They must be fed antibiotics as a matter of course. Many are no longer even able to reproduce naturally on their own.

Industrial fishing kills multiple amounts of other sea life (including dolphins and whales) to get to the specific catch being sought. With dwindling numbers due to overfishing, many fishes are now raised in factory fish farms as well, kept in extremely overcrowded and filthy water tank conditions for their entire lives until their gills are cut while fully conscious and they are left to bleed to death without a second thought.

It is not an exaggeration to say that factory farmed animals lead a life of abject misery. Not only is it not an exaggeration, it is an understatement. Such animals are commodities. Objects. Literal meat bags. And it is all fully legal. In fact, agricultural companies have been pushing for laws to criminalize the filming of animal treatment within the farm industry, labeling animal activists who simply film what goes on at factory farms as terrorists.

More than 99% of farmed animals currently come from factory farms. In the U.S. alone, about 10 billion land animals are killed for food each year. That's over 27 million land animals a day. Or almost 20,000 land animals a minute. In the U.S. alone. The number worldwide is roughly 60 billion land animals. And as high as that number is, it pales in comparison to the number of sea animals, with an estimated trillion or more sea animals killed worldwide each year.

Most of us don't know the full details of how animals reach our plate, and most of us don't want to know because it feels better if we can buy into the myth that animals lead a wonderful life except for that one very bad last day. (As we have just seen, the "wonderful life" myth is wrong on both counts. Their life is the opposite of wonderful, and most are killed while still children or young adults, so they haven't even lived a life either.) Oftentimes, even vegetarians are not aware of the full extent of the conditions in which animals are treated. Many people become vegan when they find out. It is hard to comprehend; it's almost like the dystopian imaginations of a science fiction movie.

Is Slaughter a Harm?

As we have just seen, animals in factory farms suffer in the form of severe confinement, severe overcrowding, discomfort, pain, terror, deprivation of sunlight, deprivation of exercise, genetic mis-engineering, forced breeding, separation of mother and child, living in their own filth, living in sickness, branding, castration, beak cutting, and other bodily harm without anesthesia. They are deprived of their natural tendencies and the complex social structures they would have if they were living their own life. They also suffer from boredom and insanity. These are intelligent animals who are higher up on the evolutionary scale. Pigs are one of the smartest species on the planet.

Animals on family farms suffer to a lesser degree than their factory farm counterparts, but nevertheless they are subjected to many routine painful practices including the same branding, castration, and other bodily harms without anesthesia, as well as forced breeding and separation of mother and child. Not to mention they are still enslaved, exploited, and sent off to slaughter at a very young age.

There is also no question that the trip to the slaughterhouse, and the factory slaughter line, causes tremendous pain and suffering as well. Even animals from family farms are legally mandated to be transported to slaughterhouses and virtually all slaughterhouses are factory farm style slaughterhouses. Not only is there great pain involved, but many of the animals can sense what is coming and suffer great fear and anguish accordingly.

But hypothetically, what if animals were raised on utopian farms and were killed painlessly? Or because even a hypothetical utopian farm still would involve enslavement and exploitation, what about hypothetically painlessly killing an animal in the wild? Would the killing itself constitute a harm?

Surprisingly, there is actually some philosophical debate about whether killing itself is a harm if it can be done painlessly. Some philosophers, including Peter Singer, hold that if an animal has no autobiographical sense, then killing them is not a harm if it can be done painlessly. Singer holds that position with mentally impaired humans as well, so at least his position is consistent in that regard.

Many others, and we strongly share their view, hold that killing constitutes an irrevocable harm, even if it can be done painlessly. Killing deprives a sentient individual of their entire future existence, all future possibilities, all future joys, all future experiences, and all future offspring. In the wild it could also affect entire family units, leaving children orphaned and unable to take care of themselves. There is plenty of evidence of animal grief as well. The notion that an animal with no autobiographical sense has no interest in his or her own life seems ludicrous. Animals go to great lengths to try to stay alive; they obviously want to live. And while they may not write their deepest thoughts in journals, they do have memories and levels of temporal self-awareness. We are only displaying our human-centric prejudices when we completely discount animals in this way.

Yes, it is true that humans generally plan more for the future and thus could lose more if killed, but that just means that painlessly killing a human is a greater harm than painlessly killing an animal. It does not mean that painlessly killing an animal is not a harm. This seems to be another case of answering the wrong question of "If you had to painlessly kill one of the two, should you painlessly kill the human or the animal?" rather than the real question of "In your normal day-to-day activity, should you ever painlessly kill a human or should you ever painlessly kill an animal?" where our answer should be "Neither."

There are even some humans with brain damage who are able to live fully in the present but are unable to make plans for the future. Obviously we would still consider killing them to be an irrevocable harm, even if we do it painlessly. The same should apply to animals. Dogs and cats don't have our autobiographical sense – is killing them painlessly not a harm?

Of course there may be times where it might be appropriate to kill, such as euthanizing to end a life that will only know severe pain. But for any other sentient being with a conscious will of their own, the act of killing obviously constitutes an irrevocable harm.

Should We Eat Animals?

Before finally answering this question, we should first remind ourselves of our deep-seated historical bias toward thinking that animals exist for the sake of man. We should also be aware of an even deeper bias. Since most people eat animals, we are further biased because of our deep personal investment in the matter. It *must* be okay to eat animals or else it means we are doing something morally wrong. And not just a little wrong. A lot wrong. But we're good people, so we can't be doing something morally very wrong. It must then be the case that eating animals is justified.

With that in mind, let us attempt to answer.

The strong rights position would clearly be against eating any products made from animals. The right to the individual animal's life and liberty belongs to them and it is not ours to take from them just because we want to eat them. All sentient animals have the right to not be our property. As normal as animal agriculture may seem to us at the moment, it is all animal slavery, exploitation, and slaughter and none of it is morally justified. Being against prejudice demands that we be against speciesism, and justice demands that animal slavery must finally be recognized as unacceptable, just as human slavery has finally been recognized as unacceptable. Justice owed to the animals demands that we should be vegans and not eat any products made from animals.

The position of equal consideration would be against any form of farming of animals that entails inflicting any pain and suffering. For those who held a position that painless slaughter is not a harm (despite the highly dubious logic of such a position), they might be open to products coming from hypothetical pain-free farming techniques. However, given that almost all products made from animals currently come from factory farming, and even family farming employs many very painful techniques, and all animals end up in painful trips to slaughterhouses, the position would currently also have to be a fairly strong position of not eating any products made from animals.

Now even for critics of animal rights who support the sliding scale position despite its many logical flaws, the case against products made from animals is still extremely strong. Enslavement, exploitation, forced breeding, torture, mutilation, and an early slaughter for the animal versus our taste and habit simply should not match up in any rational equation.

But here again we see a major flaw in the sliding scale model, in that it is totally open to our own bias. Would it lead one to not eating any products made from animals? Or would it lead to eating only fishes because they are further down the evolutionary scale? Or would it be fishes and birds? If one is completely intellectually dishonest, one could just say that even all factory farming is okay because animals are "so far inferior that they had no rights which the human was bound to respect."

We should also note that things are even more complicated than a sliding scale model would suggest. For example, cows are much larger than chickens and many more chickens must be raised and killed to obtain the same amount of meat. If a sliding scale model leads one to place a cow ahead of a chicken (and our limited knowledge of the two species does not even make that decision such an easy one to make), does it also lead one to place a cow ahead of two chickens? Ten chickens? A thousand chickens? Similarly, how many fishes? As well, at what level of pain and cruel treatment would the chicken overtake the cow? Similarly again for a fish. If we were ever in a situation where these questions arose regarding humans we would immediately avoid such situations entirely. The fact that these questions arise in regard to eating animals is as good an indicator as any that we should avoid these ethical quandaries and get out of the animal-eating practice altogether.

Although the sliding scale may appear to leave some room open to eating animals depending on one's bias, there is a way to consider the matter that provides much clearer guidance here. Given that a plant-based diet is perfectly healthy, it follows that for anyone who has a choice in the matter, eating animals constitutes an unnecessary harm to them.

In fact, at a rational level there does not appear to be all that much difference between eating animals and bull fighting, cock fighting, or dog fighting. One might immediately and strenuously object that they are completely different because eating animals provides sustenance and nutritional value and also is not thought of to be coming from an evil intent, but when plant-based foods are available, these differences go away. At that point, whether we are willing to admit it or not, we are simply choosing human pleasure (taste and habit in the case of eating animals; thrill in the case of bull fighting, cock fighting, and dog fighting) over unnecessary animal pain and suffering and death.

There is very real pleasure that can be derived from bull fighting, cock fighting, and dog fighting. Humans can derive pleasure from watching or betting, and it can even be a bonding experience with friendships made over it. Nevertheless, we correctly recognize that we could derive all of those same benefits from sporting events, so we correctly argue that if we have any interest in animal fighting we should train ourselves to not derive the sick pleasure from it and instead focus our attention on positive sporting events. There is no reason the same cannot be done with eating animals. We have the ability to reason and educate ourselves so that taste and habit no longer outweigh a lifetime of slavery and misery and the cutting short of the natural life of another sentient being. We can readily find new favorite dishes and create new food traditions.

In their book, *Eat Like You Care*, Gary Francione and Anna Charlton use the example of dog fighting to make a similar argument to the one presented above. Francione and Charlton convincingly argue that almost all of us currently believe that we should not impose unnecessary harm on animals, and since suffering imposed for mere pleasure, amusement, or convenience is definitely unnecessary, this necessarily leads us to a vegan diet. This is independent of equal consideration and animal rights, and holds true even if we take the sliding scale position.

It therefore appears that when we rationally consider the matter, we are inevitably led to a vegan diet. The position of strong rights, which is the position that logic dictates, clearly leads us there. But even with a speciesist sliding scale position (one that we shouldn't allow due to its numerous logical flaws), we are still led to a vegan diet. In general, one has to go all the way back to "animals are made for us to do with as we please" in order to justify eating animals. And that is exactly how the public is operating at the moment, whether they mean to or not. No matter how much a person says they love animals, their continued purchases of products made from animals unequivocally display an attitude that animals have no effective moral status at all. In this sense, many current philosophers are way ahead of the general population in recognizing that there is a strong moral case against eating animals.

In the final analysis, we would do well to always remind ourselves that the question before us is not "Who would you save in an emergency, the human or the animal?" The question is, "In my regular day-to-day living, should I ever harm a human or should I ever harm an animal?" If there are non-sentient plants in abundance that can keep us sustained and healthy, then a thoroughly compelling case can be made that "Neither, of course" should be our answer.

PART II: THE RATIONALIZATIONS FOR EATING ANIMALS

In this section we will list and examine all of the popular rationalizations people generally give for eating animals.

1. ANIMALS ARE JUST THINGS; ANIMALS DON'T FEEL PAIN

Most of us should now know that this description of animals is false. Anatomy and the theory of evolution show how non-human animals are just too similar to human animals for this theory to stand up to any reason. If animals show signs of consciousness or signs of pain, which they do in the same ways we do, the only reasonable conclusion given our scientific knowledge is that they are indeed conscious and feel pain, just as we are conscious and feel pain.

The animals we eat have consciousness. They have sentience. They feel pain. They are each individuals in their own right.

Therefore, from a moral perspective, these animals have a moral status and one would need a valid reason in order to enslave them and subject them to pain and deprive them of their life. "Because I can" or "Because I feel like it" simply does not cut it the way it would if they were just inanimate objects. Any rational moral system would require a valid reason to override their own innate subjective life and being and preferences and desires. Saying otherwise amounts to either a rationally unjustified religious statement that we have "dominion" over them, or just a blatant form of discrimination against nonhumans (known as speciesism).

That is not to say at this point that a valid reason cannot exist, but it needs to be specified and hold up to rational scrutiny.

2. ANIMALS ARE DUMB; THEY DON'T POSSESS HUMAN COGNITION

While the animals we eat are sentient, feel pain, and are way more intelligent than most of us think, they are indeed not as smart as most of us.

But why would not being as smart as us be a valid moral reason to devalue their life and pain to the point of enslaving and killing and eating them? Morality never takes that position – in fact, mistreating those below us is always seen as a hugely immoral bully trait. We certainly would never use that line of reasoning in regard to other humans.

We aren't even consistent in applying this rationalization. On the one hand, we value dogs and cats as sentient creatures and it does not matter that they are not at the same level of intelligence as us. On the other hand, we try to argue that farmed animals can be enslaved and treated as commodities and should be our food. Further calling into question our own intelligence in regard to this rationalization, we try to make such an argument concerning pigs, even though pigs are one of the smartest species on the planet, are smarter than dogs, and cats are not even on the top ten list.

Whenever we are confronted with actual footage from slaughterhouses, do we point and laugh and call the animals dumb? Most of us won't even watch. We can't bear to watch. We are sickened and turn away, recognizing the unthinkable cruelty for what it is. If we can't even bear to watch it, shouldn't that make us think that maybe, just maybe, there is something morally wrong with it? While some people are quick to dismiss such talk as simply an appeal to emotion, a slaughterhouse video is instructive because sometimes seeing something in its true form can cut away our faulty rationalizations faster than anything else. In any case, everything being said here is completely backed up by rational thought and reasoning.

Now let us consider the more formal version of this rationalization, which is the argument that animals do not possess certain higher cognitive level traits that humans possess, and that is justification enough to kill and eat them.

As we have discussed in more detail previously, this rationalization has a number of huge logical flaws. Mentally impaired humans lack these higher level cognitive traits as well. Are we justified in killing and eating them? Dogs and cats lack these higher level cognitive traits. Are we justified in killing and eating them? How would we feel about Neanderthals? Does this not mean that future evolved man and advanced space aliens are justified in killing and eating Homo sapiens? Finally, as we have previously seen, the higher level cognitive traits argument does not even answer the right question, as it answers the question of who we should save in a no-win emergency rather than how we should act on a normal day-to-day basis.

It is also quite telling that people who have made this argument have been wrong numerous times before. For example, it was once thought that language was unique to man. It was once thought that tool usage was unique to man. Could it be that we are continuing to completely discount animal abilities? Our track record is not the greatest so far.

Higher level cognitive traits are simply not relevant to the issue of killing and eating someone. They are arbitrary, irrelevant to the issue, and lead to all of the logical flaws pointed out above. Sentience, however, is relevant. All sentient beings are conscious feeling individuals who have their own wills, experience emotions, and share the ability to feel pain and suffering. The fact that you are a conscious feeling individual who will suffer pain and the irrevocable harm of losing your life if I slit your throat should be a sufficient reason for me to not slit your throat. I should not need to administer an IQ test first to know that.

Human cognition is not the relevant factor for the issue of killing and eating someone. Sentience is.

3. ANIMALS AREN'T HUMAN

Some people argue that morality toward humans is inherently different from morality toward nonhumans. But if there is such a thing as morality toward humans by definition being different from morality toward nonhumans, then there is such a thing as morality toward whites by definition being different from morality toward blacks, and morality toward men by definition being different from morality toward women.

In essence, saying that we can eat animals simply because animals aren't human is an extension of the rationalizations used to justify prejudices and atrocities against other humans throughout time. "They" are different from us. Therefore, we can completely discount their pain and life and enslave them, kill them, treat them as property or second class entities, or do whatever we want to them. It is a false rationalization for man, and it is a false rationalization for animals.

Treating beings differently based solely on species membership is a prejudice.

The word for it is speciesism.

4. HUMANS ARE OMNIVORES

Although there is some debate as to whether humans should be classified physiologically as herbivores rather than omnivores, humans clearly have the ability to eat meat and other products made from animals. But having the ability to do something is not a moral justification for doing it. From a moral perspective, the question is not if humans *can* eat animals, it's if humans *must* eat animals.

So the pertinent question is not if humans are omnivores, but rather if humans are obligate omnivores, who are obligated to eat both plants and animals. And the answer is no, we are not. We are able to eat animals, but we also do not need to include meat or other products made from animals in our diet in order to live a perfectly long and healthy life.

Why is the distinction between omnivore and obligate omnivore important? Because being able to do something is not a moral justification for doing it. We evolved fists that are able to punch. We evolved the physical ability to steal, rape, and murder. Our brains have evolved the ability to wipe out the world many times over in a nuclear holocaust. Is it moral to do those things simply because we evolved the ability to do them? Do we say we *must* do them and we were "made to do them" because we evolved those abilities? Of course not, so why would we suggest that our ability to eat animals gives us the moral authority to do so? Eating animals, just like punching, stealing, and blowing up the world in a nuclear holocaust, is a choice.

This rationalization is also an appeal to nature, as the assumption being made is that because we are scientifically classified as omnivores it must mean that it is moral for us to eat animals. However, such an appeal to nature is a fallacy in reasoning known as a naturalistic fallacy. Because something is natural does not automatically mean it is moral and good. Many things that are "natural" (including theft, rape, and murder) are extremely immoral, and we will discuss this further in Chapter 7.

Finally, some people assume that a scientific classification of humans as omnivores means that we must need to eat animals to survive or stay healthy. However, that does not follow from the scientific classification. The term omnivore only refers to a capability of eating both plants and animals, rather than a necessity of doing so. The question of whether we need to eat animals to survive or stay healthy is a related but separate question, which we will discuss in the next chapter.

Before we leave this chapter though, it is important to point out a rather disturbing quality about this rationalization, in that it attempts to make morality disappear altogether. We shall actually see this with most of the other rationalizations as well. There appears to be this strong desire to take the eating of animals outside of morality altogether, as if once the rationalization were true then morality would magically disappear. For example, most people who provide this rationalization do not argue that while it provides them a justification to eat animals, one must only eat the minimum necessary for survival and one should go as far down the evolutionary scale as possible and take great care never to buy products that came from factory farms, and so on. No. The position generally taken is that we should be able to eat as much as we want, however it reaches our plate, and from all of the animals that we are currently accustomed to eating. Morality has magically disappeared. Eating animals is now outside of morality altogether. This is a strong indication that the person is simply trying to rationalize what they are currently doing without having to actually think about it.

5. HUMANS NEED TO EAT ANIMALS TO LIVE

As far as meat goes, hundreds of millions of vegetarians and vegans around the world and throughout history may cast a little doubt on that statement. Tens of millions of vegans (and growing fast) are living healthy lives without dairy and eggs either.

Now, one may argue that in certain extreme situations humans need to eat animals to live. That may indeed be true, and would provide a moral excuse for someone who lives on, say, a deserted island. In a life and death situation, we have an excuse to do what we have to do to survive (and it should be noted that some people would eat other humans if it came down to it as well). But for the vast majority of us, where everything is available and our hunting and gathering consists solely of picking up items off of shelves at the supermarket, that moral excuse goes away entirely.

One might also argue that while humans may not need to eat animals to live, they do need to eat animals to stay healthy. This is categorically not true. The Academy of Nutrition and Dietetics (formerly the American Dietetic Association) has stated unequivocally that vegan diets are appropriate for all stages of life. Not only are responsible vegan diets healthy, but studies have shown that excessive animal consumption is the leading cause of many major diseases and ailments and statistically decreases one's lifespan. As Dr. Joel Fuhrman states in his book *Eat to Live*, there are "more than 3,500 scientific studies involving more than 15,000 research scientists reporting a relationship between the consumption of meats, poultry, eggs, and dairy products and the incidence of heart disease, cancer, kidney failure, constipation, gallstones, diverticulosis, and hemorrhoids, just to name a few health problems."

We have no desire to argue over health studies, however, and shall assume for argument's sake that eating animals in moderation is not unhealthy. This book is not here to argue over what diet is the absolute healthiest for humans while ignoring the moral dimension of the matter. Therefore, we shall simply take the research studies and the position of the Academy of Nutrition and Dietetics and other major medical bodies to show that responsible vegan diets are also healthy and leave it at that.

It is important to note, though, that there is a ton of misinformation out there about nutrition. For example, it is quite easy to get enough protein from plants, and health problems can arise from eating too much protein. Another example concerns vitamin B12, which is actually produced by microorganisms such as bacteria living in the soil or in an animal's gut. It is true that vegans have to be careful to get enough vitamin B12, but this is easily done with nutritional yeast and other fortified foods or by taking a vitamin supplement, which is no different than anyone else eating fortified foods and taking a supplement. Non-vegans who are not careful about their diet are deficient in many more vitamins than B12. And farmed animals themselves are routinely fed food that is fortified with numerous vitamins and minerals, including B12. In any case, with just a little knowledge, it is easy to live a very healthy and long life without eating animals. Many famous world-class athletes and academics eat vegan diets.

However, we have been brought up being told that we need to eat animals to be healthy, and we are inundated with animal industry advertising and lobbying efforts telling us how important animal consumption is to our diet, which creates fear and drives people to irrationality. Therefore, it is important to take our examination one step further.

WHAT IF HUMANS NEEDED TO EAT ANIMALS TO STAY HEALTHY?

Let us now examine from a moral perspective the hypothetical situation where humans needed to eat animals to stay healthy.

Morality is not an all-or-nothing affair. For example, just because there are some justifiable reasons for killing a human does not suddenly mean that homicide is outside of morality. So hypothetically if one had to eat animals to stay healthy, it does not suddenly mean that eating animals is outside of morality altogether.

If nature has a gun to our head, as it were, to force us to eat animals to stay healthy, is the gun to our head to eat more animals than we need to be healthy? No, of course not. Is the gun to our head to eat not only fishes, but also birds and mammals? No, it is not. Is the gun to our head to torture the animal as well? No, it is not. Is the gun to our head to exploit and kill animals for fur, leather, entertainment, or other non-essential purposes? No, it is not. And if the gun were ever removed from our head (say through scientific advancements, vitamins, and fortified foods) should we still go about our business as if the gun were still to our head? No, of course not.

In essence, even if nature had a gun to our head to eat animals, a moral principle of "minimization of harm" would still apply. To see why such a minimization of harm principle is a logical moral requirement rather than something optional, consider a situation where someone has a gun to our head and is forcing us to commit a crime. Suppose that the crime, however, is completely up to our choosing. Would one say that we can commit whatever crime we want, or are we still under a moral obligation to try to minimize our harm even though we are being forced to do some harm? Would we go out and murder a large family, or would we, for example, jaywalk across an empty street, steal a penny from an open cash register, or illegally download a very wealthy artist's song off the Internet? As much as we may try to take animals outside of morality altogether, we will never succeed because it is faulty thinking. No matter what, morality always remains.

Unless we (irrationally) held that animals have no moral status, we would only have the moral excuse to eat the minimum amount of animal products required to stay healthy, and not a whole lot more. And it is at this point where the sliding scale would come into play. We would have the moral imperative to seek out animals with the lowest sentience, intelligence, and ability to feel pain. For example, can we get what we need from plants and fishes? If so, then there is no excuse for birds or mammals. In fact, can we get what we need from plants and bivalves (e.g., clams, oysters, scallops, and mussels, which are much lower on the evolutionary scale and have no central brains or central nervous systems)? If so, then there is no excuse for fishes, birds, or mammals. Furthermore, the treatment of anyone we kill and the minimization of their pain and suffering would still have to be of prime importance to us. Does any of that even remotely resemble our current eating practices and farming methods?

To repeat, this was all just a hypothetical, because the fact is it is not a requirement to eat animals to be healthy. Studies consistently show this, and millions and millions of people around the world are living healthy vegan lives at this very moment. But even if one is living under an irrational fear, hardly anyone is scaremongering about a vegetarian diet, and who out there is saying that we require anything more than plants and fishes? So the obvious question to anyone with such a fear is why aren't they at least vegetarians who only eat a small amount of eggs or dairy, or pescatarians who only eat a small amount of fishes (or better yet, bivalves), and who don't exploit or kill animals for any other non-essential purposes?

Just as we saw earlier (and we will continue to see for most of the rationalizations collected in this book), once we can convince ourselves that we are justified in eating animals, we assume that eating animals goes outside of morality altogether. We simply take it for granted that we can eat all of the animals that we are currently accustomed to eating, in any quantities, and it does not really matter how the animal was treated either (at least not enough for us to stop buying). No matter how much we may say we love animals, our actions show that we think animals were made for us to do with as we please, and we do not really consider them to have any moral status at all.

Our actions therefore do not stand up to rational scrutiny even when we claim that we need to eat animals to stay healthy. Virtually no one who claims to need to eat animals to stay healthy is making any rational attempt at any minimization of harm. Virtually no one is attempting to get what they claim to be missing from bivalves. And virtually no one is stopping to exploit and kill animals for any non-essential non-food purposes. It is thus abundantly clear that we are either very confused on the matter, or we are simply trying to rationalize what we are currently doing without having to actually think about it.

6. WE'RE THE TOP OF THE FOOD CHAIN

This argument is commonly presented as, "My ancestors didn't claw their way up the food chain so that I could be a vegan!"

First, we should note that this argument means we can kill and eat dogs and cats, and we can kill and eat Neanderthals, and also that future evolved man and space aliens can kill and eat us.

We should also note that anyone giving this argument would most likely soil themselves if a lion were charging at them. And that same sentence would hold true replacing lion with tiger, bear, ape, elephant, rhino, hippo, alligator, jackal, and on and on and on. Most of us are in fact afraid of spiders and mice.

At its core, though, this argument is simply that *might makes right*, which holds very little weight from a moral perspective, and in fact usually indicates that the person making the argument is morally in the wrong.

Historically speaking, this is similar to the notion of The Great Chain of Being, which placed whites and men higher up on the hierarchy of creation than women and other races. People used that notion to legitimize human slavery, racism, and sexism. It appears we apply a similar thought process in regard to animals by appealing to nature and food chains today.

It is rather disheartening to see how many people actually provide this rationalization for eating animals. In a sense, it is an indication of just how precarious civilization is, and how quickly people are able to fall back down to their basest levels. With all of the progress we have made over the centuries, humanity still has a long way to go.

This rationalization is also an appeal to nature, which we have already pointed out is a fallacy. There is a lot more to say on the topic in the next chapter.

7. IT'S NATURAL;
ANIMALS EAT OTHER ANIMALS

First, many animals do not eat other animals. It is interesting how we so often want to lump all animals together as if they are not individual species, and individuals within each species. Nevertheless, the fact that carnivores and omnivores exist in nature does not hold any weight from a moral perspective.

Should we live naked in the wild because it's natural? Should we throw our feces as some species naturally do? Why are we only choosing to emulate the eating of animals?

Domination and fighting is a natural occurrence in the wild. Theft is a natural occurrence. Rape is a natural occurrence. Infanticide and cannibalism are natural occurrences with some species. It is hard to imagine that someone realizes the full implications of what they are saying when they put forward this rationalization.

Given that animal advocates are often accused of equating animals with humans, this rationalization is also quite telling. Most animal advocates do not fully equate animals with humans. But someone who is putting forward this rationalization for eating animals is doing exactly that. Are we just animals? Is that really the moral world in which we wish to live? The morality where might makes right? The morality of evolution's survival of the fittest? We don't hold that argument when it comes to morality. We have already seen the term for such faulty thinking – it is called the naturalistic fallacy.

We don't steal regardless of the fact that it is natural. We don't rape. We don't murder. We don't kill the old and sick and weak. We don't dominate anyone weaker than us. We clearly are not thinking this through if we are using this rationalization to eat animals.

Furthermore, are we even aware that this thought process has been used before to justify human slavery and male dominance over women? After all, some male animals dominate female ones in nature, and some animals have domination hierarchies and caste systems in nature. Apparently, we have just reinvented sexism, racism, and human slavery.

It is again rather disheartening when so many people use the fact that lions eat zebras, for example, as justification for eating animals. If lions eating zebras is the reason to take animals outside of our moral framework, why did it take both the lion and the zebra out of our moral framework? Why didn't it just take the lion out? Apparently we actually side with the "killer" carnivore and use that as justification to exploit and kill the "innocent" herbivore. And we want to call that moral?

Morality is not about what animals do in the wild, it is about what people do in a civilized society.

8. ANIMALS AREN'T MORAL; THE LION WOULDN'T THINK TWICE ABOUT EATING YOU

Some people argue that our morality should not extend to animals, as animals are not moral themselves. But since when did acting morally only apply toward other moral beings? If we came across a long lost tribe of savages, are we allowed to enslave or kill and eat them? This exact same rationalization has been used in the past for slavery and countless atrocities throughout history. "But they're just savages. They're not moral." Or, "Look at their savage religion. They must be converted or killed."

It is true that animals are not equivalent to humans and can not fully be taught to be civilized, but was that really the determining factor? If we can't teach a savage then it is justified to kill and eat them? Is it justified to kill and eat mentally impaired humans? Babies? The senile? Psychopaths? Dogs and cats? Can future evolved man or space aliens who live by a more advanced moral code use this same rationalization to kill and eat Homo sapiens?

Once again, morality is not about what animals do in the wild, it is about what people do in a civilized society.

Philosophically speaking, the idea that morality only extends to other moral beings is related to what is known as the social contract theory. The social contract theory is the view that morality comes from an agreement between people on how society should work. The implication in regard to animals is that because animals are unable to agree to create a social contract with us, then we humans do not have to extend our morality to them. However, many people have correctly pointed out that the social contract theory is a deficient theory in a number of respects even as it relates to humans, including for example in regard to sexism and racism. For our purposes, we can see that it is also a deficient theory in regard to mentally impaired humans and non-human animals.

A better philosophical approach is to consider both moral agents (people like us who have the capacity to make proper moral decisions) as well as moral patients (those who cannot, including mentally impaired humans as well as non-human animals). It is clear that our morality can and does extend to moral patients and not just other moral agents.

As a final remark, we should note that we don't even eat lions. We eat peaceful animals who mind their own business and have never attacked any of us.

9. HUMANS ARE AT THE TOP OF THE EVOLUTIONARY SCALE

If being more evolved is a valid moral justification to kill and eat someone, then does that mean a more evolved being has the right to kill and eat us? Do we root for the space aliens in alien invasion movies? Can we kill and eat dogs and cats? Would it be okay to kill and eat Neanderthals if they were still around? When man evolves in the future, will they have the right to kill and eat Homo sapiens?

One of the most popular comic books ever written is X-Men, a story about mutants who are born with super powers. The mutants represent the next stage of human evolution, but they are shunned and persecuted by their parents and society when people find out they are different. One of the reasons it resonates so much with readers is that all of us feel different and misunderstood and persecuted at some point in our life. In the comic book, Charles Xavier starts a school for mutants and trains them as superheroes to work toward a time of mutants living in peace with mankind.

However, when we use the evolutionary scale as a rationalization for eating animals, we are taking a completely different moral position from the X-Men story. We are actually rooting for Magneto and the Brotherhood of Evil Mutants, who believe it is their right to take over the world. Shall we say to ourselves, "Hey Magneto, don't just try to take over the world. Go ahead and eat humans. It's okay. You're more evolved. It's your right."

Being more advanced on the evolutionary scale is not a moral justification in its own right. Other factors related to the specific stage of evolution are what is really important. Is the being sentient with his or her own conscious will and desires? Does the being feel pain? Are there other options available to eat that are much lower on the evolutionary scale? Those are all important questions to ask beyond simply whether the being is higher or lower than us on the evolutionary scale.

10. WE'VE BEEN EATING MEAT SINCE THE BEGINNING OF TIME

Actually, humans have not been around since the beginning of time. And not eating meat is not a new thing either. People who did not eat meat have existed throughout history too.

But regardless, because something has been done by the majority a certain way until now is not a valid moral justification for anything. Up until 150 years ago, there was human slavery "since the beginning of time." Up until less than 100 years ago, women could not vote "since the beginning of time." Civilization advances. Society becomes more enlightened. Conditions change over time.

In olden days, it was possible there could have been a valid moral excuse for some people to eat animals if they were in a position of needing it for strict survival. But it has never been so easy to not eat animals as it is today. Now there are stores and supermarkets that offer aisle after aisle of every food one could possibly imagine. Any previous excuse is gone. To paraphrase Matthew Scully from his book, *Dominion*, what were once "necessary evils" are no longer necessary, so what does that leave?

Finally, if what was actually meant was that because humanity has been eating animals for so long suggests we biologically evolved to require it, we have covered that area already. Science shows that we do not need to eat animals to live healthy lives, and tens of millions of people are doing it as we speak. A person who thinks that we need to eat animals to be healthy is living in a fictitious fear-based world, but irrationality and fear is not an acceptable moral justification for anything. And once again, even with that irrational fear it still would not mean that morality on eating animals would go out the window altogether.

11. WE WOULDN'T HAVE EVOLVED BIG BRAINS IF OUR ANCESTORS HADN'T EATEN MEAT

Some anthropologists have hypothesized that the eating of meat allowed early man to obtain more energy with less effort, thus allowing for the evolution of smaller stomachs and larger brains.

Meat-enthusiasts have of course jumped on this theory, but they are incorrect to believe that it provides any valid moral justification for eating animals. First, we should note that this is a theory and not proven fact. There are competing theories. Other scientists find a much more convincing case that the introduction and cooking of calorie-rich starchy foods such as early grains and potato-type vegetables played a key role in human brain development. Yet others point to different factors entirely, such as becoming bipedal, or becoming more social, as the main cause of larger human brain development. And perhaps there were a variety of factors that played a role, rather than just one.

Second, saying that something played a role in our past does not prove anything about the present or future. If animal consumption played a role in the past, where is the evidence that animal consumption continues to be necessary in the present? Some studies even show a correlation between not eating meat and a higher IQ (although of course correlation does not imply causation). Whatever happened in the past, it is clear that we now have the ability to be healthy and smart on plant-based diets. Everything we could possibly need is readily available to us.

In fact, we now have the ability to create improvements. Evolution is not a process that happened once a long time ago and then just stopped. If we are going to evolve even bigger brains in the future according to this theory, it is most likely going to involve scientific and technological advancements in nutrition, such as fortified foods, vitamin supplements, protein bars, and health shakes, and those fortifications can easily be plant-based. Eating animals is irrelevant. People who continue to eat animals without fortifying their meals will be left in the dust according to this theory.

Finally and most importantly, however, regardless of whether the meat theory is correct or not, it is entirely irrelevant to the subject of morality. So, for the purposes of argument, let us hypothetically assume that the meat theory is correct.

Domination, rape, and murder played a large role throughout human history. Does that make them moral? Suppose we determined that people who dominated or raped or murdered others were more successful in passing down their genes and thus played a role in shaping human evolution. Would that mean domination, rape, and murder are moral? Would it mean that domination, rape, and murder get to be placed outside of morality altogether, the way it is being suggested for eating animals? Do we get to say that domination, rape, and murder is what made us the way we are today and therefore we do not need to concern ourselves with questions about their morality? Imagine if we used this same line of reasoning for other things. Subjugation and war is what made this country, so subjugation and war must be morally okay.

There is absolutely no valid moral justification in this rationalization for eating animals, even assuming this debatable theory is correct.

12. EVOLUTION – THE PALEO DIET

Some people have put forward the idea that we should eat lean meats because it was what cavemen ate. They say we should eat the same diet that cavemen ate because supposedly we evolved on that diet for 2.5 million years, so it must be the diet our bodies are evolutionarily best-adapted towards eating.

This diet is called the Paleo diet and it says things like meat is great for you as long as it is lean meat, and bread and wheat and cereal should be avoided because grains are a relatively recent addition to the human diet and our bodies are not evolutionarily adapted to them yet. Not only does the Paleo diet say to eat animals, it says to eat animals at almost every meal.

There are two problems with the Paleo diet. The first is that it once again conveniently ignores morality, and we will get to that later. The second problem with the Paleo diet is that it is faulty. It is simply misguided pop science.

Why do we say that? Because it displays a severely misguided understanding of what evolution can tell us about diet. If one were to characterize the Paleo diet in a way that highlights some of its flaws, one might characterize it as follows:

1. I know with perfect knowledge exactly what the diet was for everyone on the entire planet for the past 2.5 million years.

2. My perfect knowledge of what everyone ate over a 2.5 million year period is "proof" for what the "best diet" is even though that is a mischaracterization of evolution and

evolution makes no such claim.

3. My "proof" trumps the actual evidence-based science of today and the decades of research that completely contradicts my claims.

You see, when talking about diet, an argument that appeals to evolution can only be very limited because that is not really what evolution is about. Evolution is not about "the best diet" – it is about adaptations and their effectiveness in passing on genes to the next generation. A long-term unhealthy diet can survive and thrive from an evolutionary perspective as long as it does not get in the way of passing on genes to the next generation.

For example, we could even hypothesize that in prehistoric times it was evolutionarily advantageous to make it to procreation, to be around further in order to help the next generation achieve procreation, and then to die soon after your peak years so you are not a burden on the family group. Maybe that is what the Paleo diet is good at accomplishing. Of course, we're no evolutionary anthropologist and this would just be a hypothesis, but that is the point. So is claiming that the Paleo diet is the best diet. *It's a hypothesis.* The next step must be to go and test it out with real evidence-based science and long-term large-scale health studies to see if there is any truth to the hypothesis or not.

But wait, aren't there decades of health studies out there already which show more and more conclusively every year that the healthiest diets contain little to no meat? And that bread (especially whole grains) is perfectly fine for the vast majority of people who do not suffer from wheat allergies or celiac disease? Unless and until they can provide a large body of new long-term large-scale health studies all showing how those original studies were wrong and how great the Paleo diet is, there goes their hypothesis.

Beyond the mischaracterization of what evolution can tell us about diet, the Paleo diet is flawed on other counts as well. For example, the amount of meat our paleolithic ancestors ate is highly in dispute. As well, the animals that existed in prehistoric times are to a large degree different from the ones that exist today. Also, early grains were in fact available at least tens of thousands of years prior to the beginning of agriculture and civilization over 10,000 years ago. As well, rather than 10,000 years being an insignificant time to effect any evolutionary changes, scientists now say it was plenty of time. In their book, *The 10,000 Year Explosion*, Gregory Cochran and Henry Harpending point out that agriculture and civilization has caused the rate of human evolution to speed up a hundredfold. The premise behind the Paleo diet is misguided and just plain flawed on so many counts. For further scientific debunking of the Paleo diet, the reader is directed to *Paleofantasy*, by Marlene Zuk.

It seems clear that part of the appeal of the Paleo diet is a desperate rationalization of eating animals (as if morality simply goes away once we can convince ourselves that we need to eat animals), but another factor may also be gluten sensitivity. That was in fact the story of Robb Wolf. In his book, *The Paleo Solution*, he writes that he was not faring well on a vegetarian diet that included lots of grains, but then felt great when he switched to a Paleo diet. But it turns out the problem was not vegetarianism. The problem was that he appeared to have celiac disease. The Paleo diet worked for him because it cut out gluten, not because the Paleo diet is the "best diet" designed for all of us by evolution. Any diet that cut gluten out of his system would likely have worked for him, including a gluten-free version of his vegetarian diet, or a gluten-free vegan diet. And certainly his experience as someone with celiac disease does not broadly apply to the vast majority of people who do not have that disease.

It is also ironic to note that people who promote the Paleo diet often promote the notion discussed in the previous chapter that eating meat was the cause of human evolution toward larger brains. For example, leading Paleo diet expert Loren Cordain writes about it in his book, *The Paleo Diet*. Now imagine if we went back to the start of Paleolithic times and applied the same principle the Paleo diet is based on. Our ancient ancestors should have said to each other that they were designed by millions of years of evolution to eat a chimpanzee-like diet. So if they had listened to people like Loren Cordain and Robb Wolf and applied the very same principle the Paleo diet is based on, our ancient ancestors ironically would never have eaten all that meat and evolved those bigger brains in the first place!

As we stated earlier, this book is not here to argue about what diet is the absolute healthiest for humans. This book is about morality, particularly with a logical bent. Much of the above discussion has been off-topic to us in that sense, but we went into it to highlight how quickly and easily people believe what they want to believe based on unproven theories. People who do well on such diets then give credit to the diet when really only some specific factors are in play. For example, they give credit to the Paleo diet when really any gluten-free diet would work for them, or they give credit to the Paleo diet when really any lactose-free diet would work for them, or they give credit to the Paleo diet when really any diet that gets them to cut back on highly processed foods would work for them. And meanwhile they act as if morality just magically disappears.

From a moral perspective, there is nothing new here. It is perfectly healthy to not eat animals. That has already been long established regardless of what any Paleo diet pop science expert tells you. And although we have not discussed it, the same goes for the Blood Type diet (which has also been debunked) or any other pop science fad diet. And even if any of these diets were "the best diet" (which they aren't), morality would not magically disappear regardless.

13. HUMANS WOULD LOSE THE ABILITY TO EAT MEAT

Some people argue that humans as a species would lose the ability to eat meat over time if everyone stopped eating it, and it is important to retain the ability to eat meat just in case of a future emergency. This is an extremely weak argument for a number of reasons.

First, one can't say with certainty that humans would lose the ability to eat meat. Evolution would not make meat inedible unless it became evolutionarily advantageous for us to not have the ability to digest meat. We might need to ease back into it, but one can't say with certainty that our ability to eat meat would completely fade away.

Second, even if it were true that humans would lose the ability to digest meat in the far-off distant future, it is not a given that this would be a bad thing. The assumption being made is that eating meat could come in handy in an emergency, so it is important for humans to retain the ability to eat meat. But any emergency would just happen to a specific few individuals who very temporarily had access to an animal but no plants. Humans as a species would never be in jeopardy in that manner. Some hypothetical catastrophe affecting a few individuals in some far-off distant future is hardly a valid argument to continue the practice of eating animals, which causes guaranteed misery and death on an actual ongoing basis for a trillion or more animals each year.

Third, while people in the present should strive to leave a better world for future generations, it is simply not logical to expect people in the present to plan for every silly hypothetical disaster scenario of the far-off distant future and base their lifestyle accordingly. And if it were expected, why should we focus on this one disaster scenario rather than others? For example, it is known that animal agriculture increases the risk of animal-to-human transmitted diseases, so perhaps we need to immediately stop eating animals to prevent the much more near future disaster scenario of a worldwide pandemic that would wipe out the human race. Or similarly it is known that animal agriculture is a top cause of climate change, so perhaps we need to immediately stop eating animals to prevent a climate change disaster scenario that would wipe out the human race. Or if we're talking about silly far-off distant future hypotheticals, maybe we need to stop eating animals because hypothetically some far-off distant future cows and pigs and chickens and fishes might evolve to wipe out humans in revenge for what we're currently doing to their ancestors.

As a final point, even if we were to give credence to the idea that it was important to retain the ability to digest meat for a hypothetical distant future emergency (and we shouldn't give credence to this idea, as described in the previous paragraph), this would only be an argument for eating small amounts of meat every few years, not for eating any and all meat at all times no matter how animals are treated in the process. And it would make much more sense to create a pill or a shot that one would take instead. The solution would not be to continue eating meat in the same quantity and manner as we do now, which is quite clearly all the person who is providing this rationalization really cares about.

We have obviously spent way more time on this rationalization than it merited, but it is truly amazing to see how when people try hard enough they can not only attempt to rationalize a moral dilemma away, but can even try to turn it into a positive moral duty. "Be good little boys and girls and eat your meat. Do it for an unlikely hypothetical disaster scenario of distant future humanity!"

A FINAL WORD ON
EVOLUTION AND NATURE

As we have seen in the previous chapters, there are numerous variations on the argument that evolution has placed us in the role of eating animals and therefore eating animals belongs outside of morality. While a very small fraction of people actively concern themselves with the treatment of animals while alive and make it a point to only buy so-called "humane" meat or only hunt animals in the wild, the act of eating animals itself is taken for granted as a simple fact of nature and therefore outside of morality.

When it comes down to it, though, one of two statements is being made. Either the person is simply saying that we eat animals as a statement of natural fact which does not require any further discussion, or the person is saying that eating animals is necessary for our health.

In the case of simply stating that we are omnivores (ignoring the fact that we are not obligate omnivores), what we are in effect saying is that we should derive our morals from evolution's survival of the fittest. This is faulty reasoning because survival of the fittest is easily shown to be a horrible moral system where theft, rape, and murder are okay as well. We do not apply the morality of survival of the fittest to domination, theft, rape, murder, or how we should treat the sick or weak or less fortunate or less intelligent among us, and similarly we should not apply it to eating animals.

In the case of stating that we need to eat animals for our health (ignoring the scientific research and the fact that millions of vegans are living long healthy lives at this very moment), what we are in effect saying is that evolution has put a gun to our heads that forces us to eat animals. This is faulty reasoning because even if it were true, eating animals would still remain within morality. If the gun is to our head to eat animals, is the gun to our head to eat more than we need to be healthy? Is the gun to our head to eat not only fishes (or better yet, bivalves), but also birds and mammals? Is the gun to our head to torture the animal? Is the gun to our head to use animals for other non-food purposes as well? And if the gun were ever removed from our head through vitamins and fortified foods, should we still go about our business as if the gun were still to our head?

Clearly the omnivore/evolution way of thinking is deeply ingrained, but nature/evolution is a morally faulty way of thinking altogether as it can justify pretty much whatever horrible things we want. The following paragraph may appear at first glance to be offensive, but be clear that we are only pointing out the similarities in thought process of the person providing their rationalization. See how many rationalizations from the previous chapters you can spot.

"Men were designed by millions of years of evolution to be sexual opportunists. As a guy, sexual desire is unquestionably deep inside my DNA. It's what makes me a man. Is it possible for a man to survive without sex or through masturbation alone? Sure, maybe that's true for some men, for a while. But a man can't thrive without sex. I get depressed when I haven't had real sex for a while. I don't feel my complete self. I don't feel 100% a man. So when I'm not getting it willingly, I listen to my body and do what my body is asking for, what it was designed for. I have nonconsensual sex. And don't tell me that I don't love women. I think it's terrible how some men treat women. I don't condone any of that. I only have humane nonconsensual sex. I buy my women the best food, the best drinks, we go dancing – you should see how happy they are. And when it's time I slip them a drug and they don't feel a thing and they're unconscious in an instant. There's no fear and they never even know it's coming. And I always appreciate their sacrifice. Before I start I always say a blessing and express my gratitude for the sexual sustenance gift that they are providing me. Listen, if you don't want to have nonconsensual sex that's your personal choice and I respect it, but please respect my right to have nonconsensual sex. Men are sexual opportunists. Period. It's simple biology. Evolution. Nature. You think the lion feels bad when he's having nonconsensual sex with the lioness?"

The reason we used sex as our example is that sex is viewed as a baser drive closer to eating, but versions of the example above could have been provided to justify theft or slavery or even murder. If we accept evolution's survival of the fittest as our starting point then that is ultimately the morals we are promoting.

Any appeal to nature and evolution is thus ultimately faulty because morally it is just not the right way of thinking on the matter. Regardless of nature and our own barbaric history, civilization is meant to take us out of the realm of "survival of the fittest" and "might makes right" mentalities and to evolve beyond them. Morally speaking, it is time to evolve beyond thinking that our base evolutionary desire gives us the right to exploit, enslave, torture, or kill others. It does not. It is a prejudice.

14. MMMMM, BACON

Most people find meat and other products made from animals delicious; there is no doubt about it. But feeling good about something does not provide a valid moral justification on its own for doing it. Without intending to be inflammatory, slave owning feels good to the slave owner, but that does not morally justify slavery, and rape feels good to the rapist, but that does not morally justify rape. As much as we may hate to admit it, the thought process behind someone saying, "I could never give up meat. It tastes too good," simply does not appear to be much different from the ignorant thought process behind someone saying, "I could never give up slaves. Who would pick my cotton?" or "I could never agree to women in the workplace. Who would make my dinner?" It simply represents a statement of desire regardless of any consequences for the victim.

If taste is a valid moral basis for being able to eat someone, then can future evolved man or space aliens use this same rationalization to kill and eat Homo sapiens? Why shouldn't we eat dogs and cats? They are in fact eaten in some parts of the world even though most of us recognize that practice to be utterly barbaric.

And why stop at dogs and cats? According to this taste reasoning, why not eat humans as well? Human meat can be delicious. Do cannibals have the moral right to roast us over a spit? As some people say about animals, "If they weren't meant to be eaten, why are they made out of meat?"

If "Mmmmm, bacon" really trumps slavery, pain, suffering, and death even when nutritious plant-based food is readily available, there does not appear to be all that much difference between eating animals and bull fighting, cock fighting, or dog fighting. In all cases we are simply choosing human pleasure (taste and habit in the case of eating animals; thrill in the case of bull fighting, cock fighting, and dog fighting) over unnecessary animal slavery, pain, suffering, and death.

Just as we should train ourselves to not derive pleasure from animal fighting and instead obtain our thrills from sporting events, we should also train ourselves so that taste no longer outweighs a lifetime of slavery, misery, and the cutting short of the natural life of another sentient being. We can readily find new favorite plant-based dishes. Taste for animals was learned as a child and it can be refined as an adult. Taste buds are not set in stone and science has shown that we can readily acquire new tastes. And if hypothetically it truly is too late for someone (which it is not), why shouldn't they at least train their children differently so that things can be different for them?

Now let us also consider the flip side of this argument, sometimes stated as: "Tofu is gross!"

Where do we get this notion that vegan food can't be tasty? Vegan food is delicious, and getting more delicious and more varied by the day. Vegan culinary skills have progressed to such a degree that some of it is even winning awards over their animal-derived competitors. There are even vegan foods that mimic the different tastes and textures of various meats and other products made from animals if one finds oneself still craving those tastes. Some of it has even fooled professional meat-eating food critics. As well, remember that most spices and condiments are already vegan.

Plus, as animal activist Gary Yourofsky humorously points

out in a famous lecture he gives to students, when we eat meat we are eating flesh, blood, tendons, muscles, and veins – do we really have the nerve to call tofu gross? (He actually goes even further, noting that milk contains pus, eggs are the "periods" of hens, and Thanksgiving turkey with stuffing is ass-bread – bread made in a turkey's ass.)

Even though there is nothing wrong with tofu, one doesn't ever have to touch a piece of tofu in their life if they don't like it. The vegan food experience is exploding and there are all kinds of different vegan foods from all over the world. If we haven't even tried them before discounting them all, isn't that a bit ignorant? The notion that vegan food is bland and tasteless is an old stereotype that holds no truth today. Vegans are hardly deprived. There are many vegan foodies. Upscale vegan cuisine was named the top food trend in 2013 by Forbes.

Regardless, because someone is tasty is not a valid moral justification to be able to kill and eat them.

15. THE ROLE OF FARMED ANIMALS IS TO BE EATEN

Some people think the role of women is to be in the kitchen. Some white people used to think the role of dark-skinned people was to pick cotton. Now, that is not meant to equate animals with humans. It is simply pointing out the logical fallacy of the argument. The word "role" does not suddenly change meaning when applied to humans, does it? Saying the "role" of something is X is not a valid argument and does not make it so. The argument is false. We are simply using human examples to make that apparent.

But if one insists on non-human examples, there are plenty. If someone in another part of the world said the role of cats and dogs is to be eaten, are we suddenly going to say, "Oh, well I guess it's okay then. That's their role there." If someone said that from now on they are going to breed elephants for food, does that give them the moral authority to breed elephants for this new role? Will space aliens have the moral authority to say that the role of Homo sapiens is to be their food? Will future evolved man have the moral authority to say that the role of Homo sapiens is to be their food?

Some people try to argue that we brought the animals into existence for the sole purpose of being food, but since when does breeding provide one with the right to do whatever they want with the offspring? Regardless of your parents' idle threats, if they brought you into this world they do not have the right to take you out of it. In fact, extra burdens are placed on them to provide you with the basics of a decent life. They don't get to enslave, torture, and slaughter you.

From any logical perspective it is obvious that this rationalization makes no sense whatsoever. What gives us the right to force these animals into these roles? It is only our stubborn clinging to the notion that animals are things made for our sake which prevents us from seeing how irrational it is.

And yet some people actually go one step further, arguing that eating animals is good for farmed animals because there would be a lot fewer of them or they might even go extinct if we stopped breeding them for food.

This is a truly shocking argument when you think about it. If something is morally unjustified, doing it on a massive scale does not suddenly justify it. It appears such people do not consider individual animals to have any moral status whatsoever.

Yes, there would be billions less farmed animals in the world if people stopped breeding them to eat. And there would be that much less pain and cruelty and exploitation and slaughter in the world as a result. And the remaining animals will do just fine on sanctuaries or will successfully revert back to the wild, in case we are worried about their extinction.

And even if it meant they would go extinct, it still would never justify enslaving, exploiting, and killing and eating them. If that were the case, we should be enslaving, exploiting, and killing and eating all the animal species on the endangered species list. And why not do the same to ethnic groups of humans with dwindling populations while we're at it? If they are in danger of going extinct, is that what we should do?

We call this the abusive boyfriend rationalization. "Baby,

I'm so sorry. I only kill you and eat you because I care about you so much. I love you so much, baby!"

16. DEATH AT A SLAUGHTERHOUSE IS BETTER THAN DEATH IN THE WILD

Can we kill and eat stray dogs and cats? Can we kill and eat the severely disabled? Can we kill and eat people with incurable cancer? Or a degenerative disease? They are going to have a worse death if we leave them alone and don't kill and eat them.

A factory farmed animal lives a life of complete misery, and even so-called "humane" family farms still employ many painful practices and send the animal to slaughter after living only a small fraction of his or her natural lifespan. If we wish to provide a result better than death in the wild, is the best we can do really just slavery and death at a slaughterhouse? How about letting the animals live free on a sanctuary? And if we are breeding billions of animals each year just for the sake of killing and eating them, then how about not breeding them all in the first place? What is giving us the right to enslave and breed them? We can only put forward this rationalization for eating animals when we maintain that animals are merely our property, made for our sake, to do with as we will.

TABLE 1 – APPROXIMATE LIFESPANS

ANIMAL	NATURAL LIFESPAN	AGE KILLED FOR FOOD
Pig	10-12 years	6 months Breeder Sow: 3-5 years
Cow	20-25 years	10-18 months Dairy Cow: 4 years Veal Calf: few days to 6 months
Chicken	8 years	5-7 weeks Egg-Industry Hen: 1-2 years Egg-Industry Male: 1 day

Slavers used to make a similar argument that dark-skinned Africans were better off being slaves in advanced countries rather than being left free in Africa. How nice of these slavers. They were doing these Africans a public service. Imagine using this argument on an African American. It is pretty safe to say it would not be received very well.

This is simply another case of the abusive boyfriend rationalization. "Baby, I'm so sorry. I only kill you and eat you because I care about you so much. I love you so much, baby!"

Shockingly, some people have taken this rationalization one step further, saying that farmed animals saw an evolutionary benefit to being taken care of by humans in exchange for their labor, eggs, milk, and flesh, and thus consented to this arrangement. In other words, they were asking for it!

17. THE WORLD WOULD STARVE IF PEOPLE STOPPED EATING MEAT

Some people have the mistaken notion that if everyone stopped eating meat, we would have to grow way more plants, which we would be unable to do and people would starve. What they fail to realize is that animals eat plants too. Way more plants than we do, in fact. Right now, the vast majority of our primary crops go to feeding farmed animals. In his book, *Meatonomics*, David Robinson Simon notes, "more than half of the world's crops are used to feed animals, not people," and, "In the United States, the top three crops are corn, soybeans, and hay. Farm animals eat 70 percent of the soybeans, 80 percent of the corn, and virtually all of the hay."

In fact, it is well documented that animal agriculture is an incredibly wasteful use of our limited resources, as well as extremely damaging to the environment. Animal agriculture is a top contributor to climate change, is responsible for massive deforestation, is a massive polluter, is misusing our antibiotics supply and creating antibiotic-resistant organisms, is increasing the risk of a worldwide pandemic, is putting a heavy strain on dwindling water resources, and is grossly inefficient to the point where there would be enough food to feed the entire planet if not for animal agriculture. In his book, *Meatonomics*, David Robinson Simon notes, "raising animal protein takes up to one hundred times more water, eleven times more fossil fuels, and five times more land," and similarly, "An American eating a hamburger uses enough grain to feed six hungry people." Many people who are not even that concerned about animal rights, but who are only concerned about humans and the planet, have gone vegan because of this fact. The United Nations has issued a report urging everyone to move toward a vegan diet.

Some people argue that we should stop feeding the animals our crops and should let them eat grass instead, but it is simply not feasible to do that at the massive scale and speed of factory farming, and such an approach still has many of the same ecological problems pointed out above. Most importantly, however, one can only even attempt to make such an argument when one sees animals merely as things and resources that were made for us to use as we see fit, with no real moral status of their own. Should we ever consider exploiting, enslaving, or killing humans based on some attempted ecological calculations? Would our answer change for mentally impaired humans?

Regardless, this rationalization is false. Not only would people not starve if everyone gave up eating animals, but the reverse is true. There would be enough food to feed the world, if not for animal agriculture. Aside from any political dimension of the issue, it would not be an exaggeration to say that people in third world countries are starving and dying because we have chosen to eat animals, particularly to excess. As John Robbins in his book *Diet for a New America* writes, "Enough grain is squandered every day in raising American livestock for meat to provide every human being on earth with two loaves of bread."

18. PLANT FARMING KILLS ANIMALS TOO

There is zero equivalence between unintentional death and intentional slavery, infliction of pain, and slaughter. Should farmers continually look for ways to keep small animals away from oncoming tractors? Absolutely. In a world where the rights of sentient beings were taken seriously, farmers would take the matter very seriously. But there is still zero equivalence between that and the intentional slavery, pain, and killing in animal agriculture.

To use an analogy, imagine a doctor who is intentionally prescribing poison trying to say, "But prescribing medical drugs kills some people too." Or a motorist who is intentionally running people over with their car trying to say, "But people driving on roads causes accidental deaths too." Or an employer who is intentionally killing workers trying to say, "But accidents in the workplace kills people too."

If we recall from the previous chapter, the majority of crops are grown to feed farmed animals, so being vegan actually reduces the amount of unintentional deaths in plant farming as well. However, some people have tried to claim that in certain locations with unusable grassland, fewer animals overall would die from grazing farmed animals than from the accidental deaths in plant farming. It turns out their calculations are wrong, but even if that wasn't the case it wouldn't make a difference from a moral perspective. If animals have moral status, then one cannot simply ignore the difference between accidental death and premeditated slavery and slaughter. Would we ever make such calculations with humans? If someone calculated that fewer humans overall would die if we enslaved and murdered a certain subgroup of people, would we say that we should go ahead and enslave and murder those people? Imagine an employer who took our earlier analogy even further to say, "If I enslave my workers I can guarantee their safety until I kill them, so I'm responsible for fewer workplace deaths than those employers who don't enslave and intentionally kill their workers." Would we accept that reasoning? Of course not.

Once again, one can only even attempt to make these calculations and equate these issues when one sees animals merely as resources that were made for us to use as we see fit, with no real moral status of their own. And so we find ourselves once more at the abusive boyfriend rationalization, claiming that we're killing and eating animals only because we care about them so much.

19. EVERY LIVING THING EATS OTHER LIVING THINGS / WHAT ABOUT PLANTS?

If "every living thing eats other living things" is our justification, is it okay to eat dogs and cats? After all, every living thing eats other living things? Is it okay to eat humans? We do not even have to limit ourselves to mentally impaired humans because every living thing eats other living things. This rationalization would also mean that space aliens and future evolved man have every right to eat us.

When we put forth such a rationalization, we are in effect saying that what we are morally allowed to kill and eat extends *equally* to all biological life. That, because we are taking biological life when we eat plants, it must also be okay to take the life of animals as well. It's all the same. It's all equal. A life is a life is a life. We have thus not only equated animals with plants in this regard, but we have in fact equated humans with animals with plants with bacteria. Do we still wish to stick with this argument?

As we discussed earlier in the book, the key difference is sentience. There is a categorical difference between biological life and sentient life. Sentient animals are individuals in their own right who have their own conscious wills and desires, and subjectively experience emotions and feel pain and pleasure. We may respect the biological life of any being, but we are not imposing our will or inflicting pain on it if it has no will of its own and does not feel pain. Non-sentient biological life reacts to stimuli, but does not have subjective experiences or a conscious will of its own, and can not be harmed in the same way as sentient life. Our moral considerations apply to sentient beings.

While we are here, let us take a look at another variation of this argument. It goes something like this: "But what about plants? Plants are alive too! You're murdering all those plants!"

Once again, this has equated animals with plants by focusing on biological life without any regard for sentience. Now, some people point to various newspaper headlines about plants responding to certain stimuli and then jump to the conclusion that plants are sentient and feel pain too. What they fail to recognize, however, is that the newspaper headlines are meant to grab our attention, whereas virtually all of the actual scientists conducting the experiments readily admit that plants are not sentient and they are only showing some interesting pre-sentient phenomena.

But let us indulge this hypothetical for a moment. It takes many times the amount of plants to feed oneself through animals than it does to eat plants directly, so instead of just eating the plants ourselves, the suggestion is that we should kill *many* times more plants to feed to the animals, *plus* then also kill the more highly-evolved animals as well? That is hardly an effective argument for eating animals. In fact, it is a highly effective argument for not eating animals.

Morality, once again, is not an all-or-nothing affair. Just because one has to eat some kind of living thing to survive, does not mean it is equally open season on all living things and anything goes. That is faulty thinking. That is not how morality (or logic) works. Morality would suggest looking at sentience. Humans are not equivalent to plants and bacteria. Animals are not equivalent to plants and bacteria. Plants do not have brains and central nervous systems, and have no evolutionary need for sentience. Therefore, we should eat non-sentient plants rather than sentient animals. In the hypothetical case that plants were also sentient (even though all signs strongly indicate they are not), we would then be in a no-win scenario of having to eat something sentient in order to live, but a minimization of harm principle would still apply, where we should minimize our harm by eating plants rather than much more highly-evolved animals (with the corresponding loss of all the plants they ate as well).

At the intuitive level, we of course already know all about the categorical difference between sentient animals and non-sentient plants, because if we were ever given a bunny, a carrot, and a knife, it seems pretty safe to say that unless we were a psychopath we would cut the carrot and feed it to the bunny. And we also intuitively know about the minimization of harm principle as well, because if we thought that carrots were also sentient but we were being forced to stab either the carrot or the bunny, we would still choose to stab the carrot rather than the bunny.

20. MOST PEOPLE EAT ANIMALS

If the number of people holding a position or performing an action is what we use to prove that position or action's validity, then should we convert to Christianity if we are not already Christian? And should we subsequently convert to Islam if Muslims have more babies and become the majority world religion? Should we become politically conservative if conservatives are in power, and politically liberal when liberals are in power?

This rationalization is clearly faulty, because the size of a group performing an action neither proves nor disproves the validity or morality of that action. To put it in the words of our parents, "If all your friends were jumping off a cliff, would you do it too?"

Now, some people are worried that because most people still eat animals it will cause too much friction with others in their life if they stop. But not eating animals does not mean we have to become an animal rights activist; it simply means that we stop eating animals. If we are worried about causing too much friction with others, such as a spouse or family members at Thanksgiving dinner, we can just refrain from mentioning the moral component of our decision and instead say that the diet makes us feel lighter or healthier or something to that effect. People who respect us, though, are likely to respect our views as long as we are able to articulate them in a clear and respectful manner.

21. I WAS BROUGHT UP EATING ANIMALS; IT'S TRADITION

As most of us know, our parents are not perfect. They can be behind the times or outright wrong on hairstyles, fashion, technology, and anything and everything else. And they can sometimes hold extremely backward prejudiced views.

Upbringing and culture can explain why we start to do something and have a really hard time questioning it, but upbringing and culture is not a valid moral basis in and of itself. Ancient cultures practiced human sacrifice, something we realize is abhorrent today. Some cultures in Africa still practice female genital mutilation, something the rest of us know is abhorrent as well.

To really see how fallacious this rationalization is, consider the case of war atrocities committed under orders. The defense "But I was ordered to do it" is not considered an acceptable defense. If being ordered to do something does not absolve us of our actions, do we really think upbringing, culture, or peer pressure does?

That isn't to say it is an easy thing to go against our upbringing, especially when it is reinforced by society at large. For example, if someone wishes to reject the religion taught by their parents from the time they were young, it is very difficult to do so, especially if all of their family and friends follow that religion as well. Or in societies where women are supposed to be subservient to men, it is difficult for people (even the women) to reject the system. They are taught from a very early age to believe that is the way things should be, and the path of least resistance in society makes it easiest to continue the pattern.

It is similar for eating animals. In her book, *Why We Love Dogs, Eat Pigs, and Wear Cows*, psychologist Melanie Joy introduces the term *carnism*, the belief system that eating certain animals is considered ethical and appropriate. This ideology is so entrenched in our society that it is essentially invisible and unconscious and internalized, and so we never even question it. We are taught from a very young age to eat the flesh and secretions of certain animals, and we are told that it is normal, natural, and necessary. We are furthermore conditioned to numb our empathy and the emotional discomfort that comes from harming these animals, as well as to disconnect the meat and other animal products from their animal source. Our entire society makes eating animals the path of least resistance.

Nevertheless, if we educate ourselves and become better informed, we are able to recognize our unconscious and internalized belief systems for what they are, and ultimately overcome them. And as more and more people make that effort, society can really change. If that were not the case, there would still be human slavery and women would still not have the right to vote.

Regardless of whether we make that effort or not, this rationalization is still not a valid moral justification for eating animals.

22. MEAT IS CONVENIENT AND CHEAP; IT'S TOO HARD

It has never been easier to not eat animals as it is today.

Regardless, from a moral standpoint we should always be willing to be inconvenienced and pay more in order to do the right thing, and it is only when we stubbornly cling to the notion that animals are things made for our sake that we can even put forth such a rationalization. If dog or cat meat was cheap and convenient, would we put forward that argument? If human meat was cheap and convenient, would we put forward that argument?

It is interesting to note that the true price of eating animals is kept artificially low only through government subsidies and the externalization of much of its true costs. In his book, *Meatonomics*, David Robinson Simon breaks down all of the ways animal agriculture is offloading its true costs onto society and misleading the public, in much the same ways the cigarette companies previously did with their products. He points out that, "For every dollar in retail sales of meat, fish, eggs, or dairy, the animal food industry imposes $1.70 of external costs on society. If these external numbers were added to the grocery-store prices of animal foods, they would nearly triple the cost of these items."

Even with such market manipulation, the notion that vegan food is expensive is completely false. It can be cheaper to live on a vegan diet than any other diet. And if we include health care costs compared to the standard American diet, it is even cheaper to go vegan.

As for convenience, by the laws of supply and demand, if

more people demand vegan options they would become more convenient. We don't get to say, "I'll wait until vegan options are more convenient." It is our lack of support that is holding back progress in the first place.

Saying that something is "too hard" is easily seen to be merely an excuse if one simply ignores the problem altogether. If someone were really trying to address a problem but truly found it too difficult, they would at least address the problem to the extent that they could. For example, they would immediately cut back on their animal consumption and work very hard toward cutting it out entirely. They might start with Vegan Mondays and expand from there. They might start with vegan breakfasts, then vegan lunches, and finally vegan dinners. They might at least be vegan at home first and then start asking restaurants if they can make vegan modifications to their meals out. They would do a little research online to see what others have done before them. They might ask others to join with them so they won't feel like they are going it alone. They would ask their food stores to stock more vegan items. And they would make it clear to their government officials that they support societal changes toward veganism.

Doing none of these things makes it clear that "It's too hard" is simply an excuse.

Thankfully, more and more people are demanding vegan options and they are already convenient and becoming even more convenient (and delicious) by the week. Compared to even ten years ago, it is practically night and day. There are also numerous cookbooks, recipe blogs, nutritional resources, and other resources that can easily be found online, in bookstores, or at the nearest public library.

It is neither expensive, nor too inconvenient, nor too hard –
it has never been easier to not eat animals as it is today.

23. PEOPLE IN THE INDUSTRY WOULD LOSE THEIR JOBS

This same type of argument has been used before to rationalize the continuation of human slavery, child labor, sweatshops, and keeping women out of the workplace. People are expected to find ethical work, not unethical work. It would be a one-time switch to convert to plant-based agricultural jobs or another line of work. This one-time switch does not have a higher weight than an ongoing endless eternity of animal slavery, misery, and slaughter. One could only say that if animals have no moral status whatsoever.

As a side note, the meat industry has one of the worst records in workplace safety, and an extremely high turnover in workers every year. Can anyone with a straight face suggest it is psychologically positive for a human to be killing and dismembering thousands of animals on a daily basis?

To learn more about working conditions within the meat industry, the reader is directed to the book *Slaughterhouse*, by Gail Eisnitz. To learn more about animal agriculture's disastrous effects on neighboring communities and the environment, the reader is directed to the book *Animal Factory: The Looming Threat of Industrial Pig, Dairy, and Poultry Farms to Humans and the Environment*, by David Kirby.

24. THE ANIMAL IS ALREADY DEAD

If we purchase products made from animals, we are effectively paying someone else to enslave and inflict the pain and suffering and slaughter on the animal. It remains every much our responsibility, regardless of the fact that we did not physically enslave or inflict the pain or kill the animal with our own hands.

The person giving this rationalization may not be aware of supply and demand. If we purchase something, or support the purchase of it, then we are promoting the further production of that thing. Suppliers constantly look at demand and increase or decrease their production accordingly. If people stop buying something, suppliers move on and find something else to produce or go into some other line of work instead.

Now, is there a moral issue with eating unintentional road kill or animals who died of natural causes? Or dumpster diving for discarded meat? As long as it is not done in a way that promotes normal forms of intentional animal production, technically the moral issue appears to mostly go away, but the same could also be said for eating a human who died of natural causes. Bon Appétit.

Wouldn't it make a whole lot more sense to simply reach the point where animals, just like humans, are no longer considered food?

25. YOU CAN'T BE 100% VEGAN

When human slavery was the norm, one could have made a similar argument. Unless we were living outside of society, it would have been difficult to be 100% slave-free. Sure, we could have avoided owning slaves ourselves, but it would have been impossible to avoid all items that contained even a small degree of slave input. Slave labor would also have been used in public and private construction. Would it make sense to tell someone who was trying to abolish human slavery that unless they stayed off the roads they're a hypocrite? Would it make sense to say that since we can't 100% avoid items made with even a small amount of slave input, therefore human slavery is morally okay and we should go ahead and own slaves?

Of course not.

What we would say is that slavery is morally wrong and we must fight for society to abolish slavery. And in the meantime we should avoid items made from slavery to the extent possible, particularly the primary owning of slaves ourselves and any products made primarily through slave labor.

Similarly in the vegan context, it is currently impossible to avoid everything in the world that contains even a tiny amount of animal-derived products. But we should still state that animal slavery and exploitation and slaughter is wrong and demand society move toward abolishing it. And in the meantime we should avoid all products made from animals to the extent possible, particularly from the primary animal agriculture industry. Both because it is morally wrong, but also in order to weaken the power of the animal agriculture industry within society.

Morality is not what society makes easy for us. If society is making it impossible to live 100% according to morality, we don't change morality in order to fit society, but instead demand changes in society so that we can live morally.

26. GOD GAVE US THE RIGHT TO EAT ANIMALS

There is really no conflict between veganism and religion. For example, the Bible contains verses condoning human slavery and genocide, as well as the eating of animals. Just as we do not feel that the Bible is commanding us to own slaves or carry out genocide today, we should also not feel that it is commanding us to eat animals today. Many religious scholars in fact argue that "dominion" over animals means stewardship rather than domination. A number of religious denominations promote not eating animals.

Now, if, despite this, someone refuses to budge on their religious interpretation to eat animals, then we have a few questions to ask. The first is whether eating animals is actually required by religion, or if it is merely optional. This is important because even a religious person would have to agree that religion does not simply absolve a person of their rational thought. Therefore, if eating animals is optional, a person is no longer bound by religion on the matter, and rationality therefore dictates that another justification is still required in order to eat animals. If eating animals is not optional, the question then becomes, is it always not optional, or are there just certain feast times where it is not optional? Outside of those feast times, rationality again dictates that another justification is still required to eat animals.

Another important question to ask is whether or not the person purchases any animal products that come from factory farms. It is entirely hypocritical to claim that religion gives one the right to eat animals, but then to proceed to ignore religious laws concerning animal treatment. Particularly with factory farming, it is an absolute certainty that religious treatment laws are being transgressed. Even the Pope (Pope Benedict XVI) has spoken out against the evils of factory farming.

A further question regarding Judeo-Christian religions concerns Bible verses that seem to make it rather clear that Adam and Eve were vegans in the Garden of Eden, and also that veganism will return in Messianic times. Veganism thus appears to be both the original ideal state of creation and also the ideal state of Messianic times. So, not only is there no conflict between veganism and religion, but veganism appears to be seen as extremely positive, desirable, and the way things ought to be. Is a person doing their religion proud if they ever dismiss veganism or cast veganism in a negative light?

In any case, we should make it clear that we only asked these questions as a way to shake up a truly dogmatic person's thinking on the matter. The bottom line is that one should never ever use religion as a way to nullify the fundamental rights of others. Religion does not give one the right to enslave, exploit, and kill others. Period. Great injustices have been done in the past in the name of religion, and we should not allow our religious interpretations to let great injustices continue today.

We would suggest any deeply religious or conservative person to read *Dominion*, by Matthew Scully. A more in-depth chapter on the topic of religion and veganism can also be found in the book *Mind If I Order the Cheeseburger?: And Other Questions People Ask Vegans*, by Sherry F. Colb.

27. IT'S A PERSONAL CHOICE

If our actions are not affecting others, we generally consider them to be a personal choice. Once our actions affect others, that is no longer true. At that point, it is not a harmless personal preference. At that point, there is a victim, and other people are allowed to speak up for the victim. One is not allowed to just say it is a personal choice and expect their opinion to be respected. A reason must be provided to justify one's actions, and that reason must stand up to rational scrutiny.

If we were a slave owner, would others not have the right to tell us that we were in the wrong? If we murder or steal, do others not have a right to tell us? If our smoking affects others, do others not have the right to speak up?

Non-vegans often accuse vegans of being preachy and smug and sanctimonious. People generally get defensive and do not like to be told when they are on the wrong side of logic and morality. The bottom line, however, is that we enslave and kill sentient animals when we don't have to. We are doing it on an unbelievably massive scale, using unbelievably cruel techniques, and negatively impacting other humans and the environment while doing it. People have every right to tell us about it and try to get us to stop. It is not a harmless personal choice. There are victims to our actions. Trillions of them.

In fact, if we force ourselves to overcome our historical bias and pretend for a moment that we have been wrong about animals and consider the scale and magnitude of what is going on around us, do animal rights folks still seem smug and sanctimonious? Or are they showing amazing restraint passing out leaflets and posting on social networks to get our attention instead of using more forceful or violent approaches?

People have every right to speak up on behalf of the oppressed. And while no one likes to feel judged, we must remember that it is not a judgement on us as a total person, but rather a judgement on the particular practice of eating animals. And it is not so much personally directed at us as individuals, but rather it is a call for collective social change and a call for justice.

28. WHAT ABOUT INSECTS? / MUST WE PROTECT ANIMALS IN THE WILD? / WHAT SHOULD DOMESTICATED ANIMALS EAT? / WHAT ABOUT ANIMAL TESTING? / ETC. – WHERE DOES IT END?

When discussing the topic of eating animals, some people bring up a myriad of questions regarding animal rights, suggesting that unless all of those other questions are answered satisfactorily we do not have to concern ourselves with the morality of eating animals and can dismiss the topic entirely.

But that is not how morality works in other situations of our lives. Is morality 100% clear regarding euthanasia? Or abortion? Or every instance of killing by the state or law enforcement? Do we say that because all of those issues are not 100% resolved that morality does not apply to killing and we can do whatever we want in any situation? Of course not. There are many situations where things are pretty clear, and other situations where things are less clear. We do not need to be able to resolve every single gray area before answering the situations that are more clear.

It is beyond the scope of this book to provide a thorough discussion of these questions, although there are some things we can note about each of them. For example, regarding insects, there are at least two distinctions from other animals that can readily be made. First, it is unclear if insects are sentient. Insects have very simple nervous systems and do not react to painful stimuli in the same ways as animals higher up the evolutionary scale, so it is also unclear if they have the ability to feel pain. If they do, it is most certainly at a level quite significantly lower than that of the fishes, birds, and mammals that we eat.

While it is unclear whether insects are sentient or not, if we are uncertain, we should probably give them the benefit of the doubt where we can, so while plants are readily available the argument can still be made that we should eat non-sentient plants over possibly-sentient insects. We also should not amuse ourselves by pulling off their legs or wings or by burning them with magnifying glasses, even if it is true that we may be inadvertently killing some of them in the course of our daily lives through walking or driving. There is a world of difference between inadvertently hitting a possibly-sentient insect with a car windshield and actively paying people to inflict slavery, pain, and slaughter on a highly-sentient animal when it is completely avoidable and other options are readily available.

The second important difference between insects and other animals is that we are often in direct conflict with insects. They invade our homes, some of them suck our blood or sting us, and they can contaminate our food and infect us with disease. Are pigs, cows, chickens, or fishes invading our homes and attacking us? We are the clear and brutal aggressors in their case.

Regarding animals in the wild, this question is made difficult because some animals are carnivores or obligate omnivores and actually require meat or else they will die. So if for example we actively protect animals from a lion, we are in effect killing the lion through starvation. But because this question is difficult does not mean we have to add to the situation either. Humans do not need to eat animals to live long and healthy lives.

Regarding domesticated animals, this question is made

difficult because humans domesticated them, so we now bear a special responsibility toward them. Does this mean we should feed them meat or other products made from animals? If we should not cause pain to animals and enslave and slaughter them for ourselves, the same reasoning would make us try to avoid doing so for domesticated animals as well. At the same time, if they need to eat animals to survive, we must acknowledge that there is a difference between ourselves and the animals we adopt.

If it is indeed unavoidable, the sliding scale might come into play and suggest using bivalves rather than fishes, birds, and mammals. Or, given that most people still eat animals, one might for now simply use the leftover scraps that non-vegans are currently throwing away. Hypothetically, another solution could be to use meat from animals who lived a happy life on a sanctuary and then died of natural causes. This may sound unhealthy, but most current domesticated animal foods use meat from dead, dying, diseased, and disabled animals that are deemed unsuitable for human consumption. Most people would be absolutely shocked if they knew where their domesticated animal food really comes from.

There is evidence that products made from animals are avoidable though, by using vegan foods and supplements which have been specially scientifically formulated for each animal's nutritional needs. One might argue against this approach feeling that we should not impose human morality on animals, but in reality domestication was already an imposition and we directly and indirectly impose our way of living on domesticated animals in all kinds of ways. Suggesting that it is not "natural" would be a fallacy as well. It either works or it doesn't. The more relevant question is simply whether or not the animal can live a long, healthy, and happy life without eating animals and is not being harmed by a vegan diet. More health studies are needed before answering that question conclusively, but there is ample evidence suggesting that dogs can live perfectly long, healthy, and happy lives on well-planned vegan diets. Cats, however, are obligate carnivores. While growing anecdotal evidence of cats living long, healthy, and happy lives on special scientifically formulated vegan diets does exist, it would be premature to make a definitive claim until sufficient cat health studies are conducted.

In any event, while this is an interesting discussion, and there are many further discussions to be had on the topic of domestication, it does not change anything in regard to the human consumption of animals. Whether or not we should eat animals is not contingent on a definitive answer concerning what we are able to feed the animals we adopt. We do not need a definitive answer to the latter more difficult question before being able to answer the former easier one.

Finally, regarding animal testing, first it should be pointed out that a great many experiments are excruciatingly painful and deadly to the animals being experimented on and yet are not even life-saving at all for humans. For example, to introduce a new brand of shampoo or cosmetic or household cleaner, tests are often performed to find out how much of the product must be ingested by animals before 50% of them die. This is cruel and pointless when the new product is just a variation of products that have been thoroughly tested before. Plus, there are now newer and better testing methods that exist.

Second, it should be noted that experimental results on animals often do not even match up with humans, so while animal testing can lead to positive results for humans, it can also lead to many negative results as well, where a drug that worked on animals turns out to be harmful to humans, or a drug that would work on humans is passed over because it did not work on animals. Adverse drug reactions are currently one of the leading causes of death among humans, and meanwhile much less money is being put into areas of prevention that would save many more human lives.

Third, and most importantly, it must be noted that from a moral perspective the mere fact that animal testing can lead to benefits for humans is not proof in and of itself for experimenting on animals. If that were the case, one could argue for experimenting on humans as well, whether it be limited to convicted felons, or severely mentally impaired humans, or some other group of people.

In the case of some smaller subset of medical testing, though, one might argue that we are a bit closer to the emergency no-win situation rather than the situation of everyday living. That is very much debatable, however, and one could also point out that if it is an experiment that we would not be prepared to test on a severely mentally impaired human then we should not test it on animals as well.

There is obviously more to be discussed and debated concerning each of these topics, and other related topics as well, but the point is that while it may be difficult to know exactly where to draw the line in some cases, that does not mean we get to draw the line wherever we want and in a clearly unjustified place. Morality does not simply go away because some animal rights questions are harder to definitively answer than others, just as the harder topics of euthanasia, abortion, and killings by the state do not make morality go away in regard to killing humans. While some animal rights questions have less clear answers than others, regardless of how we answer each of these questions they all have absolutely no bearing whatsoever on the much more straightforward question of eating animals.

It is simply unjustified to expect every gray area in regard to animals to be answered to our liking before we consider any issues of animal rights. We would not be able to consider human rights either if we held it to such impossible standards. Demanding such perfection, especially in light of all of the numerous fallacies and rationalizations we have been describing in this book, is simply unjustified. A person who argues for the status quo must realize that at the rational level there is no more status quo to go back to. Intellectually speaking, it has been completely demolished. It no longer exists.

29. AREN'T THERE BIGGER PROBLEMS IN THE WORLD?

It is not a case of either/or. Many animal rights advocates work on human rights issues as well. And, unlike the fact that we have a limited time to work on all the problems in the world, we all have the choice in our daily lives to not intentionally harm either humans or animals in terms of the food we eat. In fact, it is one thing to not go out of one's way to work on animal rights, but it is quite another to be actively and knowingly working against it through one's purchases. So the obvious question for anyone providing this rationalization is why are they not a vegan who spends their limited time working on the "bigger problems" they care most about? In most cases, the person providing this rationalization is not even doing anything to help alleviate "bigger problems" in the world. It is simply a cop-out statement.

On top of that, once one recognizes that speciesism is an unwarranted prejudice, one cannot help but recognize that animal rights is one of the most important struggles in history in terms of scale (trillions of victims) and intensity of pain and suffering and slaughter. It is also important to point out that while we have finally turned the corner on racism, sexism, and many other forms of prejudice, we have yet to turn the corner on speciesism. Society still finds speciesism acceptable. We have inherited a speciesist world that goes back thousands of years and it is still a major struggle to get people to take off their blinders, bust through their rationalizations, and really think clearly and rationally about it.

Furthermore, it is the very fact that animals are so vulnerable to humans that makes it our duty to care and fight to stop their oppression. Just as would be the case with children, the elderly, and the handicapped, we actually owe more to them because they are the most vulnerable and are unable to stop oppression on their own.

Finally, animal rights is in fact human rights. As we have pointed out earlier, animal agriculture has numerous disastrous effects on humans and the environment, from pollution, to deforestation, to climate change, to antibiotic resistance, to increasing the risk of a worldwide pandemic, to disease, to wasting our limited water supplies, to world hunger. Wars are often fought over resources. Massively wasting resources thus increases the likelihood of wars.

Animal rights is also human rights because animal rights is a struggle against prejudice. Prejudice involves devaluing the "out-group" in order to maintain benefit for the self or the "in-group". When human slavery was finally abolished, it is very telling that it still took decades for women to get the right to vote, and the struggle for women and minorities continues to this day. Humans appear naturally capable of prejudice and find it hard to let prejudices go. Human prejudice will never fully disappear until we recognize that prejudice itself in all its forms is morally wrong. Animal rights is a struggle against prejudice and it more fully enlightens us on what prejudice means and the errors in thought process behind it.

In the following chapter, we consider this last point a bit more concretely.

A FINAL WORD ON PREJUDICE

Much earlier, we pointed out that a classic thought process of prejudice is one which uses emergency no-win situations, ranks different beings based on such situations, and then applies those rankings to everyday life.

If we look at prejudice historically, we in fact find a very similar and repeating thought process that uses rankings to justify prejudice in everyday life. Consider the following paragraph taken from an 1852 New York Herald newspaper editorial speaking out against women's rights:

> "How did woman first become subject to man as she is now all over the world? By her nature, her sex, just as the Negro is and always will be, to the end of time, inferior to the white race, and therefore doomed to subjection; but happier than she would be in any other condition, just because it is the law of her nature."

This type of thought process can also be found in the writings of such famous Greek philosophers as Plato and Aristotle, and it has been used time and time again throughout history to justify human slavery, racism, sexism, and numerous other prejudices.

If we express this thought process in logical form, it seems we are repeatedly putting forward the following argument:

1. A is superior to B.

2. Those who are superior should subjugate those who are inferior.

Therefore:

3. A should subjugate B.

Historically, we have challenged this thought process only by challenging the first statement. We make society realize that A is not superior to B. People from other races are equal to whites. Women are equal to men. And so on.

That is the route we have taken so far, but that is only half the battle because Statement 2 above is wrong as well. Those who are superior should not subjugate those who are inferior. That is a despicable statement of bullying and domination which needs to be challenged and defeated.

We can now see that in our exploration of animal rights we have become more fully enlightened on what prejudice means and the errors in thought process behind it. Animal rights is thus human rights because even if our views rank animals below humans, animal rights points out that Statement 2 is wrong. And until we accept that, not only are animals not safe, but children, the physically disabled, the intellectually disabled, the elderly, and the senile are not truly safe. And until we accept that, actually any human atrocity will always remain easily within reach. Simply convince yourself that you are superior to the other.

We may not realize it, but every time we purchase or eat a product made from an animal, we are confirming that we believe in Statement 2, that those who are seen as superior should subjugate those who are seen as inferior.

30. I ONLY HUNT /
I BUY "HUMANE" /
I'M FLEXITARIAN /
I'M VEGETARIAN

In this chapter, we discuss four common ways people stop short of going vegan, and note why they are not logically sufficient. We are not equating these four categories in any way other than listing them together as common ways people stop short of veganism.

Hunting and Fishing

Even though many people dislike hunters, in a certain sense they have a point that an animal living free in the wild has led a much better life than a farmed animal. Most of us dislike hunters because they are personally able to perform brutal acts that we would never perform ourselves. Yet, we don't seem to make the connection that whenever we purchase products made from animals, we are paying others to perform even worse brutal acts and we are thus every bit as responsible for them.

We have covered many of the issues involved in hunting and fishing earlier, from depriving a sentient individual of their entire future existence, possibilities, joys, experiences, and offspring, to affecting entire family units and leaving grieving individuals without mates and children orphaned and unable to take care of themselves. Kills are also hardly ever clean, and wounded animals often escape and die a slow agonizing death. Hunting can also affect hibernation and migration patterns. And because many people still mistakenly believe that fishes don't feel pain, fishing can be an agonizing way for a fish to die.

Hunting and fishing also normalizes and promotes the act of eating animals, which thus serves to promote industrial farming and fishing, where virtually all products made from animals come from today.

For all these reasons and more, limiting oneself to hunting and fishing is not logically sufficient. Killing constitutes an irrevocable harm, even if it was theoretically possible that it could be done painlessly. Animals have moral status and that means we need a very good reason to be able to kill and eat them. We don't have any.

"Humane" Animal Consumption

First, many of the so-called "humane" labels are just marketing gimmicks that do not mean what we think they mean and don't even improve animal lives in any meaningful way. For example, "Cage Free" does not mean happy animals roaming freely outside. It almost always means tortured animals crammed pretty much as tightly in a closed shed. "Free Range" almost always means tortured animals crammed in a shed with a tiny door that allows access to a five-foot-by-five-foot area of outside concrete. "Grass Fed" almost always means grazing a couple of months a year and being tightly confined and fed cut grass the rest of the year. "Organic" only means the avoidance of chemicals and antibiotics; it has no bearing on farmed animal treatment.

In fact, most of these so-called "humane" labels generally have no industry definition or regulation, and in many cases the animal industry producer can simply fill out a form and claim whatever they want with no independent verification. All of the standard torturous industry practices take place on these farms, and all of the animals are slaughtered very young just the same. For much more on the myth of "humane" animal consumption, the reader is referred to *The Ultimate Betrayal: Is There Happy Meat?* by Hope Bohanec.

"Humane" animal consumption also normalizes and promotes the act of eating animals, which thus serves to promote factory farming, where virtually all products made from farmed animals come from today.

Finally, and most importantly, by definition there is no such thing as "humane" animal consumption. It's like saying "humane" slavery, or "humane" rape, or "humane" child abuse, and so on. Sure, it is certainly better to treat a slave better rather than worse, to torture less rather than torture more, and to knock someone unconscious before slitting their throat, but please don't expect anyone to pat you on the back for it. Slavery is slavery, exploitation is exploitation, and slaughter is slaughter. Animals have moral status and that means we need a very good reason to be able to enslave and kill and eat them. We don't have any. So-called "humane" products are ultimately about making *us* feel better, not the animals.

That is not meant to dismiss any individual's intention or action, but rather to note why the individual's action is not logically sufficient, particularly as an end-goal.

It is one thing to limit oneself to so-called "humane" animal consumption for a period while actively transitioning toward veganism, but "humane" animal consumption as a personal or societal end goal is not logically sufficient.

Flexitarianism

Is it better to be, say, 80% plant-based rather than 40% plant-based? Absolutely. The more plant-based the better.

But is it morally okay to actively and intentionally buy a slave the remaining 20% of the time? Is it morally okay to actively and intentionally kill or pay someone to kill the remaining 20% of the time? Of course not. There are some moral issues that should be avoided with great seriousness, rather than just cut back on. Would we ever use this line of reasoning about human slavery or slaughter, that we should just cut back on it rather than avoid the primary ways that are responsible for it? Would we use this line of reasoning if it was just limited to mentally impaired humans?

It is one thing to be a flexitarian for a period while actively transitioning toward veganism, but flexitarianism as a personal or societal end goal is not logically sufficient.

Vegetarianism

We have covered the many issues involved in dairy and eggs earlier, from enslavement, to torture, to mutilations, to deprivations, to forced breeding, to the direct connection between dairy and veal, to the killing of newborn male chicks in grinders, and the fact that dairy cows and laying hens are still slaughtered in the end anyway after only living a small fraction of their natural lifespan.

There are a number of reasons why vegetarianism is seen by many as a "good enough" option. One reason is that vegetarianism is often viewed as less "extreme" than veganism, although that is thankfully changing and veganism is now becoming a lot more widely known. A second reason is that people often say, "I could never give up cheese." Unfortunately, there is no difference in thought process between saying that and a meat-eater who says, "I could never give up bacon."

Another reason is that many vegetarians are not aware of how dairy and eggs are produced and may be thinking about theoretical situations rather than what actually happens in reality. A vegetarian may think that dairy and eggs could be obtained without killing, whereas one must definitely kill to obtain meat (leaving aside meat from animals who died of natural causes).

It is true that "theoretical dairy" (where cows aren't mutilated and tortured, no cows are killed, calves are not taken away from their mothers, and only a portion of milk is taken away from the calf) or "theoretical eggs" (where chickens aren't mutilated and tortured, and no chickens are killed) is categorically morally better than meat, which must involve killing. In practice, however, dairy and eggs must involve slavery, suffering, and killing, exactly as meat does. Even backyard hens come from the very same hatcheries that kill newborn male chicks. And dairy and eggs is still slavery and exploitation even at the theoretical level (besides being economically impractical).

What a vegetarian can point to on the positive side is that by cutting out meat they have cut down greatly on the overall number of animals they are responsible for killing, as the numbers add up very quickly for eating chickens and fishes and other sea animals. A flexitarian can make that statement too if their plant-based percentage is high enough, but generally speaking vegetarians have cut down the most killing among the four categories listed in this chapter. Nevertheless, dairy and eggs is still unjustified slavery, exploitation, torture, and slaughter, and so we have to ask the same questions as before. Is it morally okay to actively and intentionally buy a slave for a certain smaller percentage of the time? Is it morally okay to actively and intentionally kill or pay someone to kill for a certain smaller percentage of the time? Would we ever use this line of reasoning about human slavery and slaughter, that we should just cut back on it rather than avoid the primary ways that are responsible for it? Would we use this line of reasoning if it was just limited to mentally impaired humans?

It is one thing to be a vegetarian for a period while actively transitioning toward veganism, but vegetarianism as a personal or societal end goal is not logically sufficient.

31. THE WORLD WILL ALWAYS EAT ANIMALS, SO WHY BOTHER?

People used to say there would always be human slavery. Or that women would never get the right to vote. Some things can change when we become enlightened and learn better ways.

And even if it were true, would we say there will always be theft in the world so I might as well steal? There will always be murder in the world so I might as well kill?

It's not even a case where our impact is not felt unless everyone else does it too. Our actions are a win for the animals regardless of what the majority of people do. Even if we are in the minority not eating animals, we are still accomplishing a lot of good. Our decreased demand is preventing thousands of animals in our lifetime from being bred and killed on our behalf. As listed in *Eating Animals* by Jonathan Safran Foer, the average number per American in their lifetime is about 21,000 animals. How often is one given a chance to personally prevent suffering, harm, and death on 21,000 animals?

The fact is that legal human slavery did end, and if enough people resolve to do the right thing, legal animal slavery will end too. This rationalization is a pure cop-out and we suspect any person giving this rationalization knows it.

MEAT LOGIC

As we stated from the outset, this book is not about morality in the preachy or religious sense. What this book is really about is logic and rationality. Do our thoughts and actions stand up to rational scrutiny or not? If our thought process is failing us, can we illuminate how? Let us now take stock.

As we have seen, our rationalizations for eating animals are seemingly endless, and yet none of these rationalizations stand up to any real scrutiny. In fact, through our examination we have seen that we have to hold a number of completely irrational and highly dubious positions to try to justify our behavior, and we are also extremely inconsistent between our positions and our actions.

In many cases, our rationalizations are tantamount to the irrational position that animals (or at least the animals we assign to be food) are made for our sake to do with as we please and they have no moral status whatsoever. Or, although we may not think of it in these terms, we may instead implicitly hold the intellectually dishonest sliding scale position where man is so far superior they can effectively do whatever they want to any animal. Or if we implicitly hold a less intellectually dishonest sliding scale position, we do so even though we are unable to resolve its numerous logical flaws.

Whenever we are confronted on the issue of animal consumption and use, we immediately translate the question in our heads to a different one. Rather than the correct question of, "In your regular day-to-day living should you ever harm a human or an animal?" we instead switch the question to become, "In an emergency where you could save only one, should you save the human or the animal?" We then take our answer to the emergency no-win situation and apply our rankings to normal everyday situations, even though that is a classic hallmark of prejudiced thinking.

We readily convince ourselves that the slavery, exploitation, and slaughter involved in eating animals is normal, natural, and necessary, while the vegan position of not enslaving, exploiting, and slaughtering animals is extreme, unnatural, and unhealthy.

Over and over again, and in numerous variations, we point to the law of the jungle and evolution's survival of the fittest even though those are horribly barbaric moral credos that would legitimize everything from theft to rape to murder.

We readily buy into the fear that we need to eat animals to be healthy, despite the direct evidence and a mountain of health studies to the contrary. In effect, we claim that nature has a gun to our head to eat animals, but even if that were true, is the gun to our head to eat more than we need to be healthy? Is the gun to our head to eat not only fishes (or better yet, bivalves), but also birds and mammals? Is the gun to our head to torture the animal as well? Is the gun to our head to exploit and kill animals for fur, leather, entertainment, or other non-essential purposes? And if the gun were ever removed from our head (say through scientific advancements, vitamins, and fortified foods) it seems we are happy to continue going about our business as if the gun were still to our head.

We are able to hold prejudicial positions against animals that would be seen as blatantly discriminatory if applied to humans. We are very quick to discount animal abilities entirely even though the burden of proof should be on us and not on the animal, and we especially discount the abilities of the animals we eat. Some of us even hold the highly dubious position that death itself is not a harm to the animal.

We also readily flip flop our positions as needed, first insisting that only higher level rationality counts and animals are dumb and don't feel pain, but when challenged on that we suddenly insist that all biological life counts and all biological life is equal regardless of sentience. Suddenly we become experts on plants and insist that they are super smart and sentient and feel just as much pain as animals.

We are able to live with truly amazing levels of cognitive dissonance, treating dogs and cats as members of the family while arbitrarily designating other animals to be our food (and actually our designations are completely arbitrary as well because pigs are in fact a smarter species than dogs and cats). We dote on companion animals and can't get enough of watching cute animals on TV and the Internet, and yet we can't even seem to put the two and two together when it comes to these so-called food animals and how they reach our plate.

We even get extremely upset with people who derive pleasure from dog fighting or cock fighting, or from hunting wild animals, and we expect such people to train themselves to derive pleasure from positive activities rather than barbaric ones. Yet, we are completely oblivious to the fact that we are doing the exact same thing deriving palate pleasure from eating animals who we pay others to enslave, exploit, and slaughter for us.

To make ourselves feel better, we construct a mythical farm

in our heads where animals live wonderful happy free lives except for one bad day, when in reality the lives of animals are quite the opposite. They live in heavily constrained conditions of utter misery, are tortured and slaughtered in barbaric ways, and don't even live long enough to be considered to have lived any real life at all. We'll say that we are for more so-called "humane" animal agriculture (as if the word "humane" belongs in the same sentence with slavery and slaughter), but we just point to the possibility of this mythical happy (but still unjustified) farm and then go ahead and buy meat and dairy and eggs that come from factory farms and do not consider ourselves culpable in the matter. Or we happily buy into the fake "humane" labels that are simply marketing tools to make ourselves feel better, and do little to nothing for the animals.

We even ignore the destructive effects of animal agriculture on our own environment. And we convince ourselves that the world will starve if we stopped eating animals, when in fact just the opposite is true.

Some of us even suggest that we are actually doing good for the animals by eating them, not realizing that we are acting in the exact same way an abusive boyfriend rationalizes beating his girlfriend, saying that we are doing it for their own good and that they were asking for it.

When our position is challenged, we get defensive and try to equate unintentional killing in plant farming with the intentional slavery, exploitation, and slaughter in animal agriculture.

We suddenly forget how supply and demand works, telling ourselves that we didn't directly enslave or harm or kill the animal (even though we paid someone else to do it for us), and the animal is already dead, so what's the problem?

We conjure up every intellectually lazy excuse possible, from complaining that veganism is too hard or too expensive (even though we haven't even made any serious effort to move toward it), to saying that oppressing and killing others is a personal choice, that everyone else is doing it, it was how we were raised, there are bigger problems in the world, you can't be 100% vegan in our current society, and things will never change so why even bother trying.

We try to sidestep the entire issue by arguing that morality toward humans is inherently different from morality toward other species. But if there is such a thing as morality toward humans by definition being different from morality toward nonhumans, then there is such a thing as morality toward whites by definition being different from morality toward blacks, and morality toward men by definition being different from morality toward women. Even though historically we have displayed a clear pattern of prejudice, from racism to sexism to speciesism and many others, we always fall into similar faulty thought patterns but insist that this latest prejudice being pointed out to us is different and warranted.

We further insist on being provided with a 100% complete moral code for every aspect of animal rights, that contains not even a single gray area, even though that is not possible for morality concerning humans. Yet we refuse to budge from our status quo, even though at the logical level the status quo position has been completely demolished and no longer exists.

Finally, with all of our rationalizations, we desperately try to take animals outside of morality altogether, even though that is simply not possible. But that is exactly how we proceed. Once we are able to fool ourselves into thinking that eating animals is justified, we throw morality out the window altogether and completely ignore the fact that a minimization of harm principle would still apply. So rather than become vegetarians who only eat plants and a small amount of eggs or dairy, or pescatarians who only eat plants and a small amount of bivalves, we declare it open season on all the animals we are accustomed to eating, in any quantity, regardless of how much pain and suffering is involved in order for the animal to reach our plate. And we continue to exploit and kill animals for fur, leather, entertainment, and whatever other non-essential purposes we feel like doing as well.

With meat logic like this, are we not forced to admit that we are acting like a bunch of meatheads?

AFTERWORD

Do I expect to change anyone's mind about eating animals?

In his book, *The Omnivore's Dilemma*, Michael Pollan describes reading Peter Singer's *Animal Liberation* and desperately trying to find the flaw in Singer's reasoning about equal consideration and speciesism. After trying and trying and trying, he ultimately fails. But does this cause Pollan to give up eating animals for good? No. In the end, Pollan describes how he was able to come to terms with his meat eating because he felt that the chicken wasn't personally giving him enough of an accusatory glare when he slit her throat.

There is a rationalization for everyone if you want it bad enough.

At the same time, veganism is becoming more and more mainstream. More and more people are starting to wake up to the issue of animal rights and no longer wish to participate in the slavery, oppression, exploitation, mutilation, torture, and slaughter of animal agriculture. More films and books and articles are raising awareness on the topic. People are changing their eating habits when they learn more about this subject, and I do hope this book helps change people's minds as well.

I am, in fact, quite hopeful about the future. While the emotional argument for not eating animals had always been won, it is now clear that the rational argument has been conclusively and decisively won as well. We are quickly reaching the point where a person can no longer call themself a rational person on the subject anymore if they continue to think they have the moral right to eat animals. It may still take many years or decades, but with the rational argument finally won, I am now quite confident that eating animals will soon enough be relegated to humanity's barbaric past, as it should.

Human sacrifice used to be normal in ancient societies. In the history of civilization, it has only been about 150 years since advanced societies abolished slavery, and it has been less than 100 years that women have had the right to vote. The moral justifications for past practices should always be evaluated and reevaluated with the progress of time and the advancement to a more enlightened society.

And at our personal level, it is okay for us to realize that we have taken things for granted and never questioned them before, as long as we start to make real changes once we realize there is a better way.

NOTES

Introduction

Gallup Poll:
http://www.gallup.com/poll/156215/consider-themselves-vegetarians.aspx

Bias and Misconceptions

Our Historical Bias
Obviously, it is not possible to do justice to history in only a few paragraphs. A more detailed account of how animals have been viewed throughout different periods of history can be found in Chapter 5 of *Animal Liberation* by Peter Singer and Chapters 2-4 of *Rattling the Cage* by Steven M. Wise.

A Few Misconceptions Regarding Animals
A good introductory source for this material is Chapter 3 of David Degrazia's book, *Animal Rights: A Very Short Introduction.* More in-depth material, particularly concerning a few specific species, can be found in *Rattling the Cage* and *Drawing the Line*, both by Steven M. Wise. We also include a few relevant online links below.

Sentience
Consciousness:
http://www.psychologytoday.com/blog/animal-emotions/201208/scientists-finally-conclude-nonhuman-animals-are-conscious-beings
http://fcmconference.org/img/CambridgeDeclarationOnConsciousness.pdf

Fishes Feel:
http://www.psychologytoday.com/blog/animal-emotions/201004/fish-do-feel-pain-yes-they-do-science-tells-us

http://www.fishfeel.org/

Crabs and Lobsters Feel:
http://blogs.nature.com/news/2013/08/experiments-reveal-that-crabs-and-lobsters-feel-pain.html

Higher Level Abilities
Mirror Test:
http://en.wikipedia.org/wiki/Mirror_test

Me-self and I-self:
For a further discussion of this topic, see *Drawing the Line* by Steven M. Wise.

Animal Morals:
http://www.ted.com/talks/frans_de_waal_do_animals_have_morals.html

For much more on the emotional lives of animals, we refer the reader to *The Emotional Lives of Animals* by Marc Bekoff. While sentience rather than intelligence is the relevant criterion for morality, the intelligence and emotional lives of farmed animals in particular are unfairly maligned in order to make us feel better about eating them. To learn more about farmed animals, the reader is referred to *The Pig Who Sang to the Moon* by Jeffrey Moussaieff Masson and *The Inner World of Farm Animals* by Amy Hatkoff. We also include a few relevant online links below.

Bird Brain Is a Compliment:
http://www.youtube.com/watch?v=zsjgM_GME-Y

Dogs Are People Too:
http://www.nytimes.com/2013/10/06/opinion/sunday/dogs-are-people-too.html

Chickens Are Much Smarter than You Think:
http://www.telegraph.co.uk/science/science-
news/10129124/Chickens-cleverer-than-toddlers.html

Cows Have Feelings:
http://www.upinspire.com/inspire/408/seriously-i-never-knew-
cows-c

Cows Have Eureka Moments:
http://www.psychologytoday.com/blog/the-inner-lives-
animals/201008/it-s-time-magazine-respect-cows

Pigs Are Smarter than Dogs, but Does It Matter?:
http://www.psychologytoday.com/blog/animal-
emotions/201307/are-pigs-smart-dogs-and-does-it-really-matter

The Philosophical Basis for Animal Rights

The four categories of Moral Status, Equal Consideration, Unequal Consideration, and Strong Rights are taken from David Degrazia's book, *Animal Rights: A Very Short Introduction*, although we discuss these categories in our own way.

Equal Consideration
Speciesism:
The term speciesism was coined in 1970 by psychologist Richard D. Ryder.

Unequal Consideration – Sliding Scale
Evolutionary Scale:
It should be stressed that the evolutionary scale is only a rough scale and not a strict hierarchical scale from mammals to birds to reptiles and so on down the line. Not only do we not have enough knowledge on every individual species to construct such a strict scale, but it is unclear that such a strict scale even exists.

Chief Justice Taney:
http://en.wikipedia.org/wiki/Dred_Scott_v._Sandford

Strong Rights
It is beyond the scope of this book to discuss in detail, but there is a difference in philosophical thought between those who believe in Utilitarianism and those who believe in Individual Rights. Utilitarians don't believe in rights, per se, but rather believe in making an accounting of all the pluses and minuses to an action and acting according to what will provide the most benefits to all. Peter Singer is a utilitarian. The Individual Rights view maintains that individuals have certain rights which can not be trumped by any cost-benefit analysis involving others.

Tom Regan:
Regan applies his work to animals who he describes as subjects-of-a-life. He uses a conservative description of what this means in order to make comparisons to humans that one would be hard-pressed to question. However, as science uncovers more knowledge about animals, this description automatically extends. For example, at the time he originally wrote his book, the term subjects-of-a-life could only be conservatively applied to mammals, but now it is clear that it applies to birds as well, and it will likely extend further in the future.

Steven M. Wise:
See http://www.nonhumanrightsproject.org/

Gary L. Francione:
See http://www.abolitionistapproach.com
Francione refers to the right not to be treated exclusively as a resource for others as a pre-legal moral right.

Cetaceans in India:
http://ens-newswire.com/2013/05/20/india-bans-captive-dolphin-shows-as-morally-unacceptable/

A Few Problems with the Arguments for Speciesism

Some of the material in this section is discussed in the books by Tom Regan and also Peter Singer.

Mentally Impaired Humans
Human Morality Is a Human Construct:
The idea that morality can be fashioned arbitrarily by humans is related to the idea of moral relativism. Some people actually argue that moral arguments are simply not valid or are very weak arguments to make because they say that morality is all relative and changes over time, and different societies can have different views on what is and is not moral.

It is one thing to simply note that some moral views have changed over time or differ somewhat within different societies, which is known as descriptive moral relativism. However, once one says that moral arguments are automatically weak or can be ignored because of this, one has crossed over into a form of normative moral relativism which states that we ought to tolerate everyone's behavior even if it goes very much against basic moral principles. The problem with such a position is two-fold. First, it subjectively allows any behavior, from theft, to rape, to murder, to genocide. Second, such a view completely absolves itself of logic. Any arbitrary and prejudicial behavior can be held, but the person is asking to be excused from logical thinking and logical consistency in relation to their behavior.

If speciesism is shown to be a prejudice a la racism and sexism, and it is clear that we are violating the basic principle of equality by treating like cases differently, those are fundamental discrepancies that cannot be ignored and should mean something to anyone who values logic and logical consistency. Discounting these arguments by pointing to moral relativism is a cop out. It is saying that bigotry is fine and morality should not require any logic or logical consistency. It's simply a pseudo-intellectual way of making what is actually a prejudiced and religious statement, that eating animals is moral because our bigoted views believe it to be so and morality does not need to be consistent with logic.

Answering the Wrong Question
Some people challenge the notion that human intelligence has any relevance even in the emergency no-win situation. They argue that a mentally impaired person or a non-human animal should hold the same moral weight as an abled person even in a no-win emergency. After all, if a mentally impaired person is the one making the decision they might place more weight on someone more like them rather than someone with higher human intelligence, and similarly if a bird is making the decision they would likely place more weight on bird intelligence and bird abilities rather than human intelligence. That's the trouble with emergency no-win situations; there are no truly satisfying answers. In any case, we will not be arguing for such a position in this book, but as we have pointed out, it is completely irrelevant to the case of everyday living.

Emergency No-Win Situation:
Another equivalent way to think about this matter is to consider a Sophie's Choice. This is named after the book and movie of the same name, where a mother entering Auschwitz was forced to choose between her son and daughter, being able to keep only one and giving up the other to be killed in the gas chambers. A prejudiced thought process would create rankings based on a Sophie's Choice and then apply such rankings to everyday life. But clearly this is faulty thinking. The mother of course wants to keep both of her children and wants them both to live.

In Terms of Eating

Animal Agriculture
The material found in this section is covered in numerous books and articles. For example, the reader is urged to read such accounts as those presented in the books *Animal Liberation* by Peter Singer, *Slaughterhouse* by Gail Eisnitz, and *Eating Animals* by Jonathan Safran Foer. A few more links are included

below. We have focused on pigs, cows, chickens, and fishes, but of course many more species of animals are eaten, including turkeys, sheep, goats, ducks, geese, and rabbits.

Factory Farming:
http://www.farmsanctuary.org/learn/factory-farming/

Number of Animals Killed:
http://www.farmusa.org/statistics11.html
http://fishcount.org.uk/fish-count-estimates

The Rationalizations for Eating Animals

Tom Regan covers a number of rationalizations in his books, as does Peter Singer and Gary L. Francione. Two recent books, *Eat Like You Care* by Gary L. Francione and Anna Charlton and *Mind If I Order the Cheeseburger?* by Sherry F. Colb, cover some similar ground as well. Both are excellent books and highly recommended.

One popular rationalization we explicitly left out is "Hitler was a vegetarian." Although many of the rationalizations people give for eating animals are downright silly, we did not want to cover ad hominem attacks. Suffice it to say that Hitler was not a vegetarian (see *Eternal Treblinka* by Charles Patterson), but even if he was, who cares? There are plenty of madmen, tyrants, and mass murderers who ate animals – does that say anything about eating animals?

4. Humans Are Omnivores

The Carnivore / Omnivore / Herbivore Debate:
http://greentidings.blogspot.com/2012/09/a-comparative-look-at-carnivores.html
http://freefromharm.org/photo-galleries/9-reasons-your-canine-teeth-dont-make-you-a-meat-eater/

Rather than debate the issue, however, we assume the position most favorable to the pro-eating-animal side where possible in order to show that even when one assumes their starting positions, one is still led to irrationality regardless.

5. Humans Need to Eat Animals to Live

Justification vs. Excuse:
Gary Francione points out the difference between the word justification and excuse in this context. An action can still be unjustified although we recognize extenuating circumstances and therefore excuse it. For example, eating another human to survive after a plane crash can still be considered morally wrong even though we understand the extenuating circumstances involved.

Academy of Nutrition and Dietetics:
See Position of the American Dietetic Association: vegetarian diets, July 2009, http://www.ncbi.nlm.nih.gov/pubmed/19562864

Nutrition:
See *Eat to Live* by Joel Fuhrman, p. 160. This book also contains more information about protein, vitamins, minerals, and other nutrition and health topics, although there are many other fine vegan nutrition books and resources out there as well.

Safest Source of B12:
http://nutritionfacts.org/video/safest-source-of-b12/

Farmed Animals Supplemented with Vitamins:
http://freefromharm.org/health-nutrition/b12-magic-pill-veganisms-achilles-heel/
For example, the first item from an Internet shopping search for "cattle feed" was Essential Winning Fill Cattle Feed Bale, containing a laundry list of vitamin supplements, including B12:
http://www.valleyvet.com/ct_library_info.html?
product=0f1a2dcc-90b0-47c7-9385-1c19c2c2137d&showText=1

Vegan Athletes:
There are a growing number of vegan athletes in all kinds of different sports, and a number of them have won awards and set world records, including World Record Strongman Patrik Baboumian:
http://www.examiner.com/article/vegan-power-yells-plant-based-diet-bodybuilder-as-he-breaks-world-record

What If Humans Needed to Eat Animals to Stay Healthy

Leather:
Most people assume leather is simply a by-product of the meat industry. Unfortunately, that is not the case. It can not be thought of as simply a by-product, and many cows are killed specifically for leather as well.

Vegetarian or Pescatarian:
One could possibly make other arguments such as only eating a minimum amount of cow flesh because that would minimize the total number of animals killed, but the point remains the same. Virtually no one who claims to need to eat animals to stay healthy is making any rational attempt at any minimization of harm. Virtually no one is attempting to get what they claim to be missing from bivalves. And virtually no one is stopping to exploit and kill animals for any non-essential purposes. It is abundantly clear that people are either very confused on the matter, or it is simply a rationalization to justify eating the way they like and doing whatever they like without having to think any further on the matter.

6. We're the Top of the Food Chain

The Great Chain of Being:
http://en.wikipedia.org/wiki/Great_chain_of_being

10. We've Been Eating Meat since the Beginning of Time

See *Dominion* by Matthew Scully, page 43.

11. We Wouldn't Have Evolved Big Brains If Our Ancestors Hadn't Eaten Meat

Starch Theory:
http://news.bbc.co.uk/2/hi/6983330.stm

Bipedal Theory:
http://www.theguardian.com/science/neurophilosophy/2012/may/07/1

Social Brain Theory:
http://www.youtube.com/watch?v=eCbPDld4-l0

Higher IQ Correlated with Not Eating Meat:
http://news.bbc.co.uk/2/hi/health/6180753.stm

12. Evolution – The Paleo Diet

Robb Wolf:
See *The Paleo Solution*, Chapter 1.

Loren Cordain:
See *The Paleo Diet*, pages 40-41.

Blood Type Diet:
http://en.wikipedia.org/wiki/Blood_type_diet

Morality Doesn't Disappear:
In fact, some people who believe in a Paleo diet but still realize that morality doesn't disappear follow a veganized version of the

Paleo diet.

13. Humans Would Lose the Ability to Eat Meat

Worldwide Pandemic and Climate Change:
See notes on Chapter 17.

14. Mmmmm, Bacon

Included below are just a few links on some plant-based products gaining headlines, fooling food critics, and winning awards.

Vegan "Chicken" Fools Food Critics:
http://www.nytimes.com/2012/03/11/opinion/sunday/finally-fake-chicken-worth-eating.html?_r=0

Vegenaise Better than Mayo:
http://www.slate.com/blogs/browbeat/2013/12/27/vegenaise_vs_mayonnaise_why_vegan_substitute_mayo_is_better_than_regular.html

Making Eggs Obsolete:
http://www.businessinsider.com/plant-based-eggs-from-hampton-creek-2013-12

Vegan Cupcakes Win Cupcake Wars:
http://chefchloe.com/videos/vegan-cupcakes-take-top-honors-on-cupcake-wars.html

Top Food Trend:
http://www.ecorazzi.com/2013/10/29/high-end-vegan-cuisine-named-top-food-trend-of-2013-by-forbes/

15. The Role of Farmed Animals Is to Be Eaten

Some people actually fear the reverse of farmed animal extinction, claiming that the world would be overrun by farmed animals if we stopped eating them. This is factually incorrect – as we discussed, we breed so many farmed animals because we want to eat them. It is surprising, though, how misinformed some people are, especially when even a cursory examination would prove the absurdity of the claim. For example, we only eat a few species of animals on the planet. How come we aren't being overrun by all the other species we don't eat? And of course, even if this claim were true, which it is not, how would that give us the right to eat them? How is our first line of defense to eat? And does it not even enter such a person's mind to feed the animals some form of birth control?

Groups of Humans Going Extinct:
In fact, it seems that if someone eats farmed animals because they are worried about them going extinct then they are also committed to enslaving, force breeding, and killing and eating any groups of humans in danger of going extinct, because otherwise someone is sure to accuse them of caring more about animals than humans.

16. Death at a Slaughterhouse Is Better than Death in the Wild

Approximate Lifespans:
Sources include
http://www.compassionatecook.com/writings/an-unnatural-life-span and
http://www.baahaus.org/faqs.html
There is some variation for natural lifespans depending on the breed. Genetically mis-engineered breeds generally don't live as long. For example, the Red Junglefowl, which is a wild ancestor of chickens, can live up to 30 years.

17. The World Would Starve If People Stopped Eating Meat

See *Meatonomics* by David Robinson Simon, pages 5 and 130, and *Diet for a New America* by John Robbins, page 352. Much of the material in this chapter can be found in numerous books and articles, including *Meatonomics* by David Robinson Simon, *Diet for a New America* by John Robbins, and *Eating Animals* by Jonathan Safran Foer. We include a few more relevant links below.

Climate Change:
https://www.worldwatch.org/files/pdf/Livestock%20and%20Climate%20Change.pdf

Resources:
http://ajcn.nutrition.org/content/78/3/660S.full

Antibiotic Resistance:
http://www.youtube.com/watch?v=iLhSk_0tWJ4

Worldwide Pandemic:
http://www.theatlantic.com/health/archive/2012/08/how-industrialized-farming-could-facilitate-pandemic-swine-flu/261356/
http://birdflubook.com/g.php?id=5

UN Urges Vegan Diet:
http://www.guardian.co.uk/environment/2010/jun/02/un-report-meat-free-diet

18. Plant Farming Kills Animals Too

The motorist analogy can be found in Gary Francione's *Introduction to Animal Rights: Your Child or the Dog?*, and the drug analogy can also be found in chapter 13 of *Mind If I Order the Cheeseburger?* by Sherry F. Colb.

Farming Death Calculations:
http://www.animalvisuals.org/projects/data/1mc/

21. I Was Brought Up Eating Animals; It's Tradition

While most people are concerned with their own upbringing and traditions, some people express concern over the traditions of historically oppressed groups such as Native Americans and wonder if veganism is insensitive to those traditions. Traditions should never trump injustice in any case, but for a more detailed discussion on the topic, the reader is referred to chapter 10 of *Mind If I Order the Cheeseburger?* by Sherry F. Colb.

22. Meat Is Convenient and Cheap; It's Too Hard

See *Meatonomics* by David Robinson Simon, page 6.

26. God Gave Us the Right to Eat Animals

Pope Condemns Factory Farming:
http://www.all-creatures.org/living/howpope.html

Vegan Garden of Eden:
See *Genesis* 1:29

Vegan Messianic Times:
See *Isaiah* 11:6-9

28. What About Insects? / Must We Protect Animals in the Wild? / What Should Domesticated Animals Eat? / What About Animal Testing? / Etc. – Where Does It End?

For more on the topic of animal testing, the reader is referred to *Animal Liberation* by Peter Singer, *The Animal Rights Debate*, by Carl Cohen and Tom Regan, and *Introduction to Animal Rights: Your Child or the Dog?* by Gary Francione.

A Final Word on Prejudice

New York Harold Quote:
Tom Regan discusses this quote in Chapter 6 (page 118) of *Defending Animal Rights*, from which this chapter was inspired.
The reader should notice as well some of the similar types of arguments used in that editorial that we see today, namely: it's nature, everywhere in the world it is done this way, humans are a superior species and it is proper to use inferior species for our purposes, it always has been this way and always will be this way, and the animals are happy in their lot and a farmed life is better than death in the wild.

Plato:
For example, "...nature herself intimates that it is just for the better to have more than the worse, the more powerful than the weaker; and in many ways she shows, among men as well as among animals, and indeed among whole cities and races, that justice consists in the superior ruling over and having more than the inferior."

Aristotle:
For example, "...the lower sort are by nature slaves, and it is better for them as for all inferiors that they should be under the rule of a master."

Statement 2:
Alternatively, Statement 2 might be phrased as, "It is natural for those who are inferior to be subjugated by those who are superior" and Statement 3 as, "It is natural for B to be subjugated by A." The result is the same, namely that B is subjugated by A.

31. The World Will Always Eat Animals, So Why Bother?

See *Eating Animals* by Jonathan Safran Foer, page 121.

Afterword

See *The Omnivore's Dilemma* by Michael Pollan, Chapter 17.

An obvious question for Pollan is why does he still eat mammals? Even with his intellectually-challenged rationalization, why does the lack of a chicken's sufficiently accusatory glare apply to all animals, including mammals? Do pigs and other mammals also not provide him with sufficiently accusatory glares? Is it okay to kill and eat mentally impaired humans who do not provide a sufficiently accusatory glare? Do we each get to decide as individuals what level of glare counts as sufficiently accusatory, ignoring everything we know from science about evolution, anatomy, and sentience?

BIBLIOGRAPHY

Bekoff, Marc, *Animals Matter*, Shambhala Publications, 2007

Bekoff, Marc, *The Emotional Lives of Animals*, New World Library, 2007

Bohanec, Hope, *The Ultimate Betrayal: Is There Happy Meat?*, iUniverse, 2013

Cochran, Gregory, and Harpending, Henry, *The 10,000 Year Explosion: How Civilization Accelerated Human Evolution*, Basic Books, 2009

Cohen, Carl, and Regan, Tom, *The Animal Rights Debate*, Rowman & Littlefield Publishers, 2001

Colb, Sherry F., *Mind If I Order the Cheeseburger?: And Other Questions People Ask Vegans*, Lantern Books, 2013

Cordain, Loren, *The Paleo Diet*, John Wiley & Sons, 2011 edition

Dawn, Karen, *Thanking the Monkey: Rethinking the Way We Treat Animals*, HarperCollins Publishers, 2008

DeGrazia, David, *Animal Rights: A Very Short Introduction*, Oxford University Press, 2002

Eisnitz, Gail A., *Slaughterhouse*, Prometheus Books, 1997

Foer, Jonathan Safran, *Eating Animals*, Little, Brown and Company, 2009

Francione, Gary L., *Introduction to Animal Rights: Your Child or the Dog?*, Temple University Press, 2000

Francione, Gary L., and Charlton, Anna, *Eat Like You Care*, Exempla Press, 2013

Freedman, Rory, *Beg*, Running Press, 2013

Freston, Kathy, *Veganist*, Weinstein Books, 2011

Fuhrman, Joel, *Eat to Live*, Little, Brown and Company, 2011 edition

Harnack, Andrew, editor, *Animal Rights: Opposing Viewpoints*, Greenhaven Press, 1996

Hatkoff, Amy, *The Inner World of Farm Animals*, Stewart, Tabori & Chang, 2009

Joy, Melanie, *Why We Love Dogs, Eat Pigs, and Wear Cows*, Conari Press, 2010

Kirby, David, *Animal Factory: The Looming Threat of Industrial Pig, Dairy, and Poultry Farms to Humans and the Environment*, St. Martin's Press, 2010

Masson, Jeffrey Moussaieff, *The Pig Who Sang to the Moon: The Emotional World of Farm Animals*, Ballantine Books, 2003

Moran, Victoria, *Main Street Vegan*, Penguin Group, 2012

Patterson, Charles, *Eternal Treblinka*, Lantern Books, 2002

Pollan, Michael, *The Omnivore's Dilemma*, The Penguin Press, 2006

Regan, Tom, *The Case for Animal Rights*, University of California Press, 1983

Regan, Tom, *Defending Animal Rights*, University Of Illinois Press, 2001

Regan, Tom, *Empty Cages*, Rowman & Littlefield Publishers, 2004

Robbins, John, *Diet for a New America*, H J Kramer Inc., 1987

Roleff, Tamara L., and Hurley, Jennifer A., editors, *The Rights of Animals*, Greenhaven Press, 1999

Scully, Matthew, *Dominion*, St. Martin's Press, 2002

Simon, David Robinson, *Meatonomics*, Conari Press, 2013

Singer, Peter, *Animal Liberation*, The Ecco Press, 2002 edition

Sunstein, Cass R., and Nussbaum, Martha C., editors, *Animal Rights: Current Debates and New Directions*, Oxford University Press, 2004

Wise, Steven M., *Rattling the Cage*, Perseus Publishing, 2000

Wise, Steven M., *Drawing the Line*, Perseus Publishing, 2002

Wolf, Robb, *The Paleo Solution*, Victory Belt Publishing, 2010

Zuk, Marlene, *Paleofantasy*, W.W. Norton & Company, 2013

FURTHER READING
(AND VIEWING)

Earthlings:
http://earthlings.com/?page_id=32

Gary Yourofsky Lecture:
http://www.youtube.com/watch?v=es6U00LMmC4

Gary Yourofsky Q & A:
http://www.youtube.com/watch?v=WIkC4OJEx3c

Humane Farming Myth:
http://freefromharm.org/animal-products-and-ethics/a-comprehensive-analysis-of-the-humane-farming-myth/

Humane Meat Spoof:
http://www.theonion.com/articles/we-raise-all-our-beef-humanely-on-open-pasture-and,30983/

Melanie Joy Lecture:
http://www.youtube.com/watch?v=7vWbV9FPo_Q

Speciesism: The Movie:
http://www.speciesismthemovie.com

UN Urges Vegan Diet:
http://www.guardian.co.uk/environment/2010/jun/02/un-report-meat-free-diet

Vegan Starter Info:
http://www.chooseveg.com/
http://www.vegankit.com/

ABOUT THE AUTHOR

Charles Horn is an Emmy-nominated writer and producer with credits including *Fugget About It*, *Robot Chicken*, and *Robot Chicken: Star Wars*. He has a Ph.D. in Electrical Engineering from Princeton University.

Made in the USA
San Bernardino, CA
16 January 2015